Are you there gin?
It's me,
Mary Ann at 80.

Dear Val,
I am so glad you are getting Brock House back on its feet? I hope you enjoy reading this and have a good laugh —
Mary Ann

Are you there gin? It's me, Mary Ann at 80.

SELECTED REAL AND SECRET LIFE EVENTS OF MARY ANN

Mary Ann Carter

Copyright ©2020 Mary Ann Carter.

All rights reserved. No part of this publication may be reproduced, distributed or transmitted in any form or by any means, including photocopying, recording, or other electronic or mechanical methods, without the prior written permission of the publisher, except in the case of brief quotations embodied in critical reviews and certain other noncommercial uses permitted by copyright law. For permission requests, write to cartermaryann72@gmail.com.
Mary Ann Carter —1st ed.

ISBN 978-1-71667-153-1

My autobiography is dedicated to my daughter, Holly, my son, Steven, and my grandchildren: Rhys, Julia, and Sophie.

And any future great-grandchildren I will be lucky enough to meet!

I hope you will enjoy reading about the relatives you came from, and remember, as Mahatma Gandhi said, "The best way to find yourself is to lose yourself in the service of others."

Acknowledgements

EDITOR, POET, PROVOCATEUR, AND friend, Judyth Hill, helped and stimulated me to want to keep writing until my autobiography was finished. Her energy, enthusiasm and support made this happen for me.

She had me get in touch with Mary Meade for the layout of my book. Mary has been a delight to work with. She clearly explains what she needs to do and suggestions she has.

In one of the writing courses I took from Judyth in San Miguel, I met Duane. I can't thank him enough for the information he provided me with to help me learn more of my family's historical information.

It turns out my friends from the University of Minnesota - Dee and Nick - and Duane's children, went to school together and the children still stay in contact with one another! How unbelievable is this?

My college roommate of four years, Cricket, kindly offered more information for my chapter of our college years. What a treasure she is!

Another English major college classmate, Carol, offered other superb suggestions for the college chapter. Many thanks, Carol.

Vancouver friends, Susan and Trish, supported me throughout this process.

Younger, childhood family friend, Marty, remembered me helping her adjust to junior high school, remembered my zorch attack, and the party my parents had playing pin the breasts on the woman. When Marty sent this information to me, I was grateful to add it to my autobiography.

Marty's brother-in-law, Ross, was totally encouraging of me to complete this and remembered his father-in-law thinking of my father as being the smartest of the Wauwatosa group.

I thank my sister, M.J., for sharing her memories of being with our Aunt Mary, when M.J. was young.

My life-long friend Claire's description of me for this book, as she remembers me, is wonderful. We've been friends for close to eighty years.

Lynne, my eldest niece, wanted to make sure I noted her as being my "favorite niece." When you live with one another, even for a short period of time, and have similar occupations and genes, of course, you become "the favorite"! And Lynne tried her best to find her grandfather's obituary in the Milwaukee Journal. No luck.

My second husband, Ian, is a special treasure for me. He offered me total support in a variety of ways to help me complete this autobiography. He gave me pictures and reminded me of experiences I had forgotten about, to include in this book. He took time away from his other interests to help work on the book's cover.

My step-daughter, Emma, provided me with correct dates, information, encouragement, and appreciation.

My son, Steve, wondered how I would describe him. He, too, provided numerous pictures for my book and the encouragement to get it done.

My daughter, Holly, let me know my writing was getting better, she enjoyed what I was writing, and she helped share information about her grandfather. She was totally supportive of me getting my autobiography in print.

I send total thanks and hugs to all of you.

Contents

Acknowledgements . . . . *vii*

Chapter 1: My Ancestors 1

Chapter 2: Mother Mynnette Eloise Lomas Sheller 5

Chapter 3: My Father, Albert Foster Sheller 17

Chapter 4 : Childhood Memories-
The Good, The Bad and The Ugly. 25

Chapter 5: College and Early Work History 39

Chapter 6: Pre-Marriage History. 47

Chapter 7: Seven Year Marriage History with First Husband 51

Chapter 8: My Life as a Single Parent…
Or Some of the More Interesting Parts of It. 61

Chapter 9: Early Life with Ian 71

Chapter 10: Adjusting to My New Marriage in the '80s. . . . 77

Chapter 11: The Carter's Life in the '90s 83

Chapter 12: Mary Ann's Running and the Pink Sweater . . . 89

Chapter 13: P.E.O. 97

Chapter 14: My Musical Life 105

Chapter 15: Marijuana, Mary Ann and Music 109

Chapter 16: My Health 113

Chapter 17: The Carters In Mexico 119

Chapter 18: Is Retirement Fun? 139

Epilogue 143

About the Author 145

CHAPTER 1

My Ancestors

Don't judge me by my relatives.
~ Seen on T-shirt

FAMILY RESEARCH IS NOT boring.

I became inspired to write a family history for my children and grandchildren when I realized there were many things I wish I had known about my own parents and grandparents.

When my father retired, he became very interested in his heritage. He traced our ancestors back to the 1600's! He recorded nine generations, starting with Johannes Scheller, who was born in Switzerland. Johannes suffered religious persecution by the Catholics because he was an Anabaptist and was exiled to Otzweiler, Germany with his family in 1675.

His son, John Christian Scheller, was born around 1704. It is amazing to learn family details from almost 300 years ago.

Son John married Maria Catharina Ubel on January 24th, 1729 in Becherbach, Germany. Coincidentally, my father's birth date was January 24th. Maria gave birth to their first born, Johann Heinrich Scheller in 1730 and two years later, in 1732, to Daniel.

Are you there gin? It's me, Mary Ann at 80.

The family emigrated to Lancaster County Pennsylvania in 1749 and received a land grant for farming. They arrived at the Port of Philadelphia on a ship called *THE ISAAC* on September 27th, which coincidentally is my birth date.

I was pleasantly surprised to find a listing of *THE ISAAC's* male adult passengers on the internet. John's name is spelled Johann Christian Schiller. The internet researcher said many of the passengers could not spell their own names and some of their Germanic speech was difficult to understand, so the passenger listing on the arrivals has numerous errors.

There is no listing of any women or children on the ship. This seems to me to reflect how inconsequential women and children were thought to be in those days.

How long do you think it took to cross the Atlantic?

The average time was seven weeks. Passengers suffered illness, cramped quarters, food and water rations, and death. When someone died, they were thrown overboard as there wasn't enough room on board to stow bodies.

Johann Heinrich was seventeen, Daniel was fifteen and John and Maria were about 45 years old when they arrived in Philadelphia aboard *THE ISAAC.*

Imagine the pioneering spirit of these Anabaptist ancestors, bravely leaving their familiar village lives. Sailing across the Atlantic Ocean to a country where they don't speak the language or understand the customs. And possibly may be subjected to further religious persecution.

What possessions, if any, did they bring with them? Did they wear just one set of clothing? Being a religious family, I imagine they brought a Bible. Were they scrawny after their arduous sea voyage? How did they get to their property? How did Maria deal with her periods? How did the passengers deal with elimination? They didn't have toilet paper.

Think of yourself doing something like this. What adventuresome people they were!

Another item: Heinrich is listed as being an inmate in 1789, 1801, 1803 and 1807. I wonder what offense(s) he was accused of committing? Were the offenses related to being an Anabaptist? Was Heinrich a bit of a rebel as he was born on Halloween? Did the American's celebrate Halloween then?

Daniel is listed as being a shoemaker. He died in Washington County, Maryland in 1801. Did Daniel move to Maryland to escape his brother's foul reputation? Was he still an Anabaptist?

There is more detailed information about the Sheller family not recorded in this chapter in *Sheller Family Trees of America*, Parks M. Adams, R. and Paula Sheller Adams, 1998. One of the things that stood out for me from this tome is the number of children the families had. Many had seven or eight.

I did some research about Anabaptist Mennonites. They are not Amish, among other differences. The only clothing standard Anabaptists use is modesty.

Anabaptist Mennonites are a Christian movement dating back to Priest Menno Simons in the 1500s. He was a Catholic priest but started doubting many Catholic beliefs. Priest Menno had the courage to stand up for what he believed in and questioned Catholic tenets.

In reviewing the Bible, Menno did not think infants should be baptized. He believed adults should be baptized. He left the Catholic Church in 1544 and the term Mennonites was used by those who followed Menno.

He left Switzerland because of persecution. His brother was killed because of his Protestant beliefs. I don't know if any of my relatives were killed but they were exiled from Switzerland to Germany because of religious persecution.

Are you there gin? It's me, Mary Ann at 80.

Anabaptists are proponents of peace, justice and non-resistance. Perhaps this is in our DNA.

My daughter confronted a gang of boys on a street who were bullying another young male.

My son wanted to be a Canadian. He didn't want to be drafted.

Anabaptists did not enlist during the wars and did not pay the part of their taxes that would go to supporting the military. I wonder why they were not arrested or fined for disobeying this tax law.

Today, there is disagreement between some Anabaptists sects regarding homosexuality. My family believes in tolerance for all.

There are 2.1 million Anabaptists in the world in 87 countries.

To think many of us have their genes! What a blessing!

I believe we need to stand up for what we feel is right, not through violence but with peaceful actions as our ancestors did.

CHAPTER 2

Mother Mynnette Eloise Lomas Sheller

I am who I am. Your approval is not needed.
~ Seen on T-shirt

MARY FARNSWORTH, MY MOTHER'S mother, was born in 1879 in Cresco, Iowa to Mr. and Mrs. John Farnsworth. I was unable to find Mary Farnsworth's name in any Cresco high school records. I wonder if she was tutored or went to a private school.

She attended Northwestern University in Evanston, Illinois, for two years. It is amazing to think of a young woman in the late 1800's attending an educational institution when women did not even have the vote. Hooray for her parents.

Their family belonged to the Methodist Church. Her father told her she had to return to Cresco as he couldn't afford to pay for her college education and contribute to the building of the new Methodist Church.

She obeyed her father, returning to Iowa. However, her rebellious nature was evident as she joined the Congregational Church.

Are you there gin? It's me, Mary Ann at 80.

Frank Baird Lomas was born in 1896. He was three years older than Mary. After graduating from Cresco High School in 1894, he went into the hardware and coal business with his father. His graduating class consisted of five boys and five girls.

Mary Farnsworth and Frank Lomas were married by Rev. J. Ridlington, an old friend of their family. They were married in 1901. Mary was twenty-two and Frank was twenty-five. They were married in the spacious front parlor of Mary's parents' home.

Mary and Frank were both popular and esteemed young people according to a news article written about their wedding. She was "exquisitely costumed in white", carrying pink and white roses. To quote, "The bride is an accomplished and refined lady. She is modest, unassuming and cultured in attractive, domestic and social acquisitions."

"Mr. Lomas is one of Cresco's most prominent and active young businessmen."

As part of the ceremony, Miss Laura Rose Mead played the bridal march as the couple waltzed down the stairs to their wedding and heard "O Promise Me" played as part of their ceremony.

The wedding guests were surprised by the appearance of Cresco's newest band who serenaded the bridal party at the reception.

The newlyweds went on a two-week honeymoon to the Pan American Exposition in Buffalo, New York. They took the 9:15 train for Milwaukee, WI, then the boat through the Great Lakes to Buffalo on Lake Erie.

Following the birth of their three children, Mary had her teenage sons make a jelly cupboard for her, using fruitwood from their property. My mother had this cupboard in their dining room for years. It is now a refinished antique wood cupboard with new doors in our condo.

As my sister and I were growing up, we would often visit our grandparents in the summer. I slept in the hot attic where there were many books. I think Grandma Mary read palms. Reading her palmistry books fascinated me. I used to wonder if this opportunity led me to want to be a psychologist.

Frank was an active Republican; he was the representative of Howard County, from 1929-1931. He was twice president of the Iowa Retail Hardware Association. He belonged to the Masonic Order and was a member of the Congregational Church. He gave much service to his community. He was appointed Country Manager and had a siren on his car. My sister and I loved it when he would blast away. Sometimes he sounded it in their own neighborhood. The children would all run home as if they were caught doing something naughty.

Frank worked at an abattoir when I was quite young. I wasn't thrilled visiting his place of work as it smelled dreadfully. I could

Are you there gin? It's me, Mary Ann at 80.

also hear the animals making scary noises before they were slaughtered. I'm surprised I didn't become a vegan.

We never called him Grandpa, but "Daddy Frank." As he grew deaf, Mary would shout, "Frank, FRANK." I can still hear her. I shared this with my sister, and she seconded my thought.

On one of their visits to Wauwatosa, Daddy Frank had a heart attack while we were sitting at our kitchen breakfast table. He fell to the floor. I was told to go to my room. I don't remember what else happened, but he lived many more years.

After he retired, they moved to Lakeland, Florida. They had a grapefruit tree in their backyard, and I loved having fresh grapefruit every morning when we visited. Grandma Mary would find neighbor children around my age for me to play with.

Daddy Frank died of a heart attack, in 1961, at the age of eighty-five. Soon after that, Grandma Mary moved back to Cresco, Iowa.

She helped finance a nursing home in Cresco and after moving in, felt like it was "her home." She had a private room and bath. One of the residents started coming into her room at night. This intrusion bothered her. My mother brought her a water gun and told her to squirt the woman when she entered. It only took two nights, two squirts, before the intrusions stopped.

In 1971, I was living in Coquitlam, British Columbia, with my two young children, separated from my first husband. It was early in the morning. I knew Grandma was sick. I was standing next to my grand piano and I saw her face and heard her say, "Mary Ann, everything will be alright, everything will be alright." I started to cry but felt better inside myself.

That same day, my mother called me from Iowa at ten a.m. and said my Grandma Mary had died. She was ninety-two years old. During her lifetime she experienced getting indoor plumbing, learning to drive a car, electricity, television, telephones, airplanes, computers, rockets and a man walking on the moon. How many changes have you experienced in your life?

Mary Ann Carter

I wish I could have written the following letter to my mother before she died:

Dear Mom,

I remember you hated your middle name, Eloise, and seldom used it.

You were born in 1904 in Cresco, Iowa, a small mid-west farming community, and you had two brothers. Baird was older, and Craig was younger. While in college, Craig died from the flu epidemic in the 1920's.

There was a storage barn on your property, but you never had large animals. You only had dogs. You never had cats as a cat once frightened you and you never got over your fear.

One day, you told me you were exploring the attic of the barn and found a wash tub with rotting fruit in it, smelling very alcoholic. You found an old, scruffy boot in the corner and plopped it into the brew. You said both of your brothers gave you dirty looks that night at dinner. Obviously, they couldn't say anything to you nor could you to them, but what might they do in revenge? Somehow you never finished telling me what might have happened as a consequence of you "booting the booze." I still can picture you doing this.

I just loved hearing about your life as I was growing up. Most homes had outhouses, not indoor plumbing. The outhouse you used as a child was still on the property when we visited our grandparents, but they had indoor plumbing. On Halloween, the older children would often put the school outhouse on the school roof, as a joke. Just thinking about doing this gives me the creeps!

When you turned 19, you joined a philanthropic association which provides educational opportunities to women. You were in this association for 75 years. In May 1999, you were honored at the state convention in Madison, WI. At age 95, you were able to stand up from your wheelchair, address the hundreds of women at the convention in a loud enough voice to be heard and thank them for the opportunities the association provided for you. I was nearly in tears and felt very proud of you.

Are you there gin? It's me, Mary Ann at 80.

I remember a summer meeting of your chapter in our house in Wauwatosa. Most of the ladies left around 4 p.m. There was a huge crystal punch bowl on a linen-covered card table in our living room. The ladies had fruit punch in the afternoon at their meeting sipping out of dainty crystal cups. Three of your friends stayed and their husbands, including my father, arrived from work around 5:30. You found a bottle of gin and poured the whole bottle of gin into the remainder of the punch. Being eight or nine years old, I was totally appalled.

You attended Coe College in Illinois for 2 years, where you were invited to join the Gamma Phi Beta Sorority. You transferred to Iowa State University (ISU) in Ames, where you met my father. You majored in Home Economics. I remember during the war you always found a way to cook inexpensive meat, other than liver, so it was tasty and tender. We would walk to the small grocery store to purchase meat using coupons for the butcher. I can still picture his bloody apron.

Foster proposed to you in the ISU Rose Garden prior to your graduation. After graduating from ISU, you took a job teaching in Cozad, Nebraska. When I think about it, I'm not sure about the number of eligible bachelors in Cozad, although you were always attractive. I think he was quite smart to propose to you before he left, to make sure you didn't hook up with someone else.

Your fiancée then went to Harvard to get his MBA. You told me you were lonely and wrote him a letter asking how long it would be before you would get married. I can imagine how long it took for your letter to get halfway across the country, be answered and returned to you.

You married in 1929, not that long after your graduation. Your wedding dress was a pink Charleston length outfit you eventually donated to a museum in Cresco. I wore it to a high school dance in Wauwatosa before your donation.

You told me when you were living in Chicago, you used orange crates for end tables in your apartment. And you would dry out the paper toweling so you could use it again. I wondered if hygiene was taught in your Home Ec course.

My sister was born in 1933; two years later you were pregnant with twin boys. One twin was born dead and the other died shortly after birth. My sister and I never knew if the boys had names, or where, or even if, they were buried. You just wouldn't talk about your dreadfully sad experience with either of us.

I remember you told me that after the twins were born you could never have any more children. In 1939, you had me. I imagine your pregnancy with me was fraught with worry. We never talked about this. All your births were caesarian, and your stomach looked a mess. You obviously always wore a full swimming suit and as I recall, those were the days when women wore girdles so your dress shape would be compact.

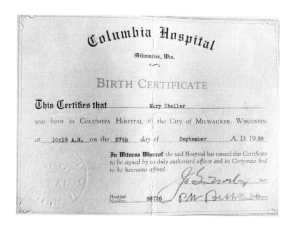

In 1949, you sent Charles Addams, a cartoonist with The New Yorker Magazine, a letter about some of my antics that appalled you. He sent you a letter dated the 28th of August 1949.

When I was in high school, I remember you telling me you tried to commit suicide between my sister's and my birth. This would have been during the Great Depression. I have no idea why you told me, and I was shocked to learn this. Milwaukee has canals throughout the city with raised bridges for the traffic on the water and land. You attempted to drive your Oldsmobile into the canal as the bridge was being raised.

Are you there gin? It's me, Mary Ann at 80.

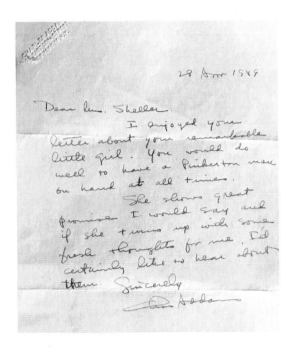

When I think of this now, it seems a foolish act for you to try as the canals were not deep. You never told me what happened or how you and the car were rescued. Or if you did, I don't remember it. I now wonder how you and my father communicated about this; I wonder what kind of intimacy the two of you shared about your feelings, or if one was just expected to keep a stiff upper lip and it got to be too much for you. Your suicide attempt seems like a plea to be comforted in your grieving.

Following this action, you found comfort from your church relationships, P.E.O. and participating as a volunteer in community activities, including being a Girl Scout leader.

You and my father lived in West Allis during the Depression and you taught home economics in night school to help with family finances. I feel you were a woman ahead of your times, as now, most women have to work to make household ends meet.

During the war, you were the block warden in Wauwatosa and needed to check all the houses on the cul-de-sac after dark to make sure the window shades were down, as Milwaukee was an industrial town and might be bombed.

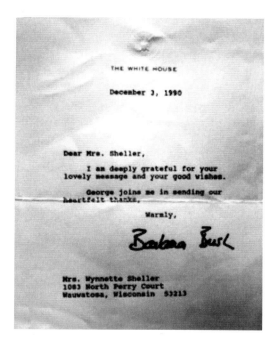

You worked for the Red Cross for many, many years. When Milwaukee became accessible to foreign ships through the Erie Canal, you set up a language interpretive center for the sailors. First Lady Barbara Bush sent you a letter thanking you for all your efforts with the Red Cross. You were very modest about this, but the rest of the family were quite impressed.

Most summers in Wauwatosa, you would make fudge and penuche to enter the cooking contest at the Wisconsin State Fair. As I recall, you usually got 1st place as your candy had great texture; it was smooth, and not overly sweet. I always wondered what criterion the judges used in sampling all the entries. If the same judges were used year after year, would they remember candy made by my mother?

Your health wasn't the greatest. You were diagnosed with uterine cancer when I was a freshman in college. One of your radiation treatments was on St. Patrick's Day and you taped a shamrock to your bum before the treatment. Many times, the two of us laughed about this.

Are you there gin? It's me, Mary Ann at 80.

In the following years, as a partial result of the early radiation, you developed colon cancer, bladder cancer, skin cancer and shingles. I always felt if you had said what you felt, you would have been a lot healthier, but this too we never talked about. On the other hand, you had a great belief in God.

My sister and I would often fly back to Wauwatosa to be supportive of you when you were receiving treatment. I remember when you needed to use a bag to urinate, I made you a few long, loose dresses. Even with all your health issues, you were always cheerful and grateful for our attending to you. You were a wonderful model for me, and I often miss you.

Much love from your daughter,

Mary Ann

Now the above is about the mother I remember as an adult. So, what about Mynnette as my mother when I was a child?

I remember when I was in early grade school my mother often drove to find me after school. She'd grab me, pull my pants down and spank me in front of my friends. I was supposed to come home right after school but playing with my friends was much more enticing. I'm not sure if I could tell time then and I certainly didn't have a watch. I've never forgiven my mother for these spankings. I felt humiliated and embarrassed in front of my friends: for 1) seeing my underwear 2) seeing my bum, and seeing me being hurt by a family member, not necessarily in that order.

I don't remember any other physical punishment from her.

My mother was very strict about what I was allowed and not allowed to do. I was a bit afraid of her. In high school all hell broke loose between the two of us. We would fight every morning before I left for school. When I came home, close to 9-10 hours later, I had forgotten we were fighting. She hadn't and was working on further arguments about why she was right, and I was wrong. This pattern went on day after day. In this day and age, I would diagnosis this as psychological abuse.

I had braces in high school. After one of my first kissing dates, I came home with swollen lips. She didn't see my lips until the morning. She burst into tears, sniveling around all day. I wanted to ask her what her problem was but didn't dare. I remember feeling guilty for having swollen lips, although I loved the previous kissing and I worried about not knowing how to kiss with braces without getting swollen lips. Because of my mother's behavior, I certainly couldn't ask her why she was so upset or how to kiss with braces. I don't think she ever had braces. I know she had a lot of tooth problems with many caps being placed on her teeth.

I returned to NYC after an accident in Nassau (see Health chapter). The following year, I found out I was pregnant, so my June wedding in Wauwatosa was moved to March in NYC. My mother had skin cancer at my wedding and sat with a handkerchief pressed up against her nose. I was upset with her attitude, and obviously she was upset with me. As the years went on, we got over our attitudes and appreciated one another. When I remarried, we both had grown up.

At age 95, her kidneys were failing, and she was close to the end of her life. I spoke with her on the 4th Sunday in November 1999 and said I would be with her in the nursing home on Tuesday; I asked her to please wait for me to be with her when she passed.

The nursing home called Monday night and said she died. I was furious with her for not waiting for me to be with her, as she was

Are you there gin? It's me, Mary Ann at 80.

with my grandmother when she died. I wanted to comfort mother in her last hours and not have her die alone. But thinking of her the way I do now, I think she would not want me to be alone with her and suffer her loss alone, as she did with Grandma Mary.

My sister and I planned a memorial service for my mother and father. Our mother felt no one would come to her funeral. Well, the Congregational Church in Wauwatosa was crowded with P.E.O.'s and relatives of the Sheller's friends.

The children we grew up with were there. Jack W. brought a movie projector and showed us family / friend slides that covered a long period of our lives when we were younger. One of our friends recalled the Shellers always having a 4th of July Party. One year, when the gang was in their 80's, mother had them play "pin the tail on the donkey." However, instead of a donkey, she had a nude cardboard breast-less female and the gang had to pin the breasts on the figure! I wonder why she never told me about this.

The children of our parents had so much fun reminiscing about them, we decided to get together every two years. We called ourselves "The G2's" or the second generation. We met in Madison and Lake Winnebago, Wisconsin; Vancouver, British Columbia; Hendersonville, North Carolina; Bradenton, Florida; Minneapolis, Minnesota; and Omena Lake, Michigan. We met over a period of fourteen years. We stopped meeting due to some of our member's age, death and inability to travel.

In our Vancouver home, there are reminders of my mother…a Christmas scarf she gave me, a pair of her red Christmas socks that still have her name label on them, a silver egg cutter, a serape she brought me from Mexico, and a mink jacket I wouldn't dare wear outside now for fear of being shot. And more important than these, I have good thoughts about her.

CHAPTER 3

My Father, Albert Foster Sheller

I may be wrong, but I doubt it.
~ Seen on T-shirt

MY FATHER, ALBERT FOSTER Sheller, was born in 1905, to Melissa Brennaman (Brenamans) Sheller and Benjamin Franklin Sheller in Lanark, Illinois. Melissa was thirty-four years old and Benjamin was forty-three years old when they married. Benjamin Sheller died January 10, 1910, when Foster was five years old. I don't know what he died of. Melissa needed to work, so she sent Foster to a farm where he would be taken care of and could help the farmer. I had a picture of him which was taken when he was around six or seven years of age, holding a hoe and wearing a pointed sun hat. The thought of my father, away from his mother and having a job as a youngster, makes me wonder how much this experience in his early life influenced him in his future life decisions and his ability to show his emotions. My sister and I used to tease him calling him a "Foster foster child." He didn't appreciate this.

Are you there gin? It's me, Mary Ann at 80.

In 1915, Melissa married a widower, Albert (Bert) Emmert, in Dallas Center, Iowa. My father was ten years old. Bert Emmert had two older children from his first marriage, Ray and Mary Emmert. Grandpa Emmert was a member of the Dallas Center United Brethren Church and did not smoke, drink or dance. My father's mother, Melissa Emmert, died August 19, 1941, when I was two years old. I have no idea what she died of. Obviously, I have no memory of her.

Foster's stepbrother, Ray Emmert, was a successful lawyer, and helped Foster financially when he went to graduate school to get his MBA. And Foster paid him back. Mary Emmert was a missionary in the Belgian Congo. She was never married. She wrote a book about her experiences. My children each have a copy of this book. When she would return from the Congo, she brought the Shellers ivory gifts. When I brought this ivory into Canada, I had a letter from my father declaring this ivory as a gift. My daughter now has most of the ivory on display in her home.

When Aunt Mary returned from Africa to stay with us, my father needed to hide his liquor supply as alcohol was forbidden in Mary's religion. My older sister and she would share our twin bedroom. When we went to bed, my sister would pretend to be asleep until Aunt Mary came to bed. Aunt Mary would kneel at the edge of her bed to say her prayers before climbing in. This totally impressed my sister.

When we visited the Emmerts, my family stayed in a motel as my father smoked cigarettes and enjoyed having a bourbon. Grandpa Emmert taught me to play checkers and consistently won every game. Then one day, I won. I was quite excited about this.

He let my sister drive his antique Model T car around the block with me as a passenger. My father dusted off the car, cranked up the engine, and off we went. All of a sudden, we heard something dragging under the car. My sister drove back to the Emmert's home and we discovered the muffler had fallen off. My sister was worried Grandpa Emmert would be furious. Grandpa Emmert didn't seem to mind as much as my father.

I know little more of my father's childhood. In fact, he and I seldom had a one-on-one conversation. I remember asking him once to tell me about his childhood, and he said, "I wasn't a very good father." I was shocked to hear him say this and we both started crying, but nothing more was said. I think it was hard for him to talk openly about his feelings because of his early losses and adjustments to three different living conditions before he was eleven years old: the death of his father, living without his mother and then living with a new father, step-brother and step-sister.

He attended Iowa State University, (ISU) majoring in Electrical Engineering. This is where he met my mother, Mynnette Lomas. He proposed to her in the ISU rose garden. I can see him on one knee with an engagement ring in his hand. My sister and I saw one of her "dance cards" and Foster's name filled most of the blanks.

In 2003, my daughter, Holly, and I sat in the same rose garden where my father proposed to my mother. Holly was in charge of two teams from British Columbia competing in the International Odyssey of the Mind Contest, held at ISU. We explored the ISU Library and unexpectedly saw a plaque on the wall, dedicated to Foster, acknowledging him for the contributions he made to the ISU yearbook called "The Bomb." He never told me about this! Holly has one of The Bomb's. His name is on the copyright as the business manager in 1926.

Foster drove a Model T Ford from Dallas Center, Iowa to New York City, N.Y., the summer before he attended Harvard. Besides telling us he had numerous flat tires, he noted it was not a good idea to stay in cheap hotels as you might get bed bugs. He parked his car in a Brooklyn field while working in NYC. You couldn't do that today! Not only did he have a job, he took extra parts in operas, as a silent extra, carrying swords, etc. I never thought he was interested in being on stage, so it was quite a surprise for me to find out he had earned extra money by taking bit parts in operas.

Are you there gin? It's me, Mary Ann at 80.

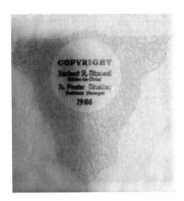

While at Harvard, he received a letter from Mynnette wondering when they would marry. I think she was lonely in Cozad, Nebraska. So, soon after he completed his MBA, he sold his Model T to a classmate and took the train to Iowa, a faster way back to Mynnette. His classmate gave Foster a check for $19 for the Model T and the classmate's check bounced!

After my father and my mother married, during the beginning of the Depression, he had a job checking gas meters in Chicago. This job was quite below what he was qualified to do. But it provided the newlyweds with money. I've seen a picture of their apartment that shows their antique clock. My husband, Ian, and I now have that clock in our condo, running on batteries.

Later during the Depression, they moved to West Allis, Wisconsin, and Foster worked for a manufacturing firm called Le Roi Company. The company made non-combustible engines starting in 1913 to 1954, when it was purchased by Westinghouse, who later sold it to Waukesha Motors in 1958.

When my parents moved to Wauwatosa, Wisconsin, Foster was employed at Phoenix Hosiery for a very long time. Phoenix Hosiery began in 1897. They made stockings and hosiery for men, women and children. They focused on the middle to upper class, but their advertising was mainly aimed at the upper class. The company was known all over the world. During 1939, Japanese silk merchants toured the company. It was sold to Kayser-Roth in 1959, following their move to produce their products at small southern locations.

During the Depression, my father did not get a paycheck but continued to work there. I wonder if he had to borrow money or how he continued to provide for us. He would walk to Bluemound Avenue and take the streetcar to downtown Milwaukee.

Eventually he left the company and did consulting around the southeastern part of the country. I wonder if he had southern contracts with some of the hosiery factories connected with Phoenix. His last job, which he really liked, was at Waukesha Motors, Waukesha, WI. It is interesting to note Le Roi Company, his first job in Wisconsin, was finally purchased by Waukesha Motors in 1958, his last place of employment. In 1968, Waukesha Motors was purchased by Bangor-Pointer. In my research, I found that my father purchased 1,450 common shares of Waukesha Motors, June 3, 1968.

In 1942, we moved from Kavanaugh Place, Wauwatosa, to a newly built house at 1083 North Perry Court. The lot backed onto a city park. I was three years old. Over the years, we had pheasants galore parading around our back yard, red and silver foxes and many different kinds of birds.

Perry Court road was dirt but was paved several years later. My patent leather shoes would get dusty when I walked home on the dirt street.

In the winter, when the snow came over the edges of the window sills, Foster would take the toboggan to the grocery store to buy food for our neighbors and ourselves. If I went with him, on the way there he would repeatedly remind me I would have to walk home on the way back, as the groceries would be on the toboggan. When I think about it now, why couldn't I sit on the top of all the groceries?

My parents had a steady group of friends they socialized with throughout the years, going to dances, concerts, sledding parties, costume parties, picnics, and entertaining in one another's homes. One of their friends told their son-in-law he thought Foster was "the smartest of the gang." I think that's probably because my father didn't talk that much!

Although my parents were very social, we had very few pictures of my father with a smile on his face unless he was drinking. He stopped smoking in his '50's after a heart attack but continued enjoying his bourbon. In his later years, my mother convinced his heart specialist to put him on anti-depressants. I believe his depression could have been caused by the circumstances of his early youth.

My parents lived on Perry Court until it was necessary for them to move into a nursing home, over fifty years later. They also had a home in Sun City, Arizona. Every winter they would load up their car and drive there. They would take the toaster, the microwave, etc. I think these choices were made because of their living through the Depression Years. They could have bought another toaster/microwave without any financial stress in Arizona. And thinking of him driving to Arizona, age ninety, gives me the willies. In Sun City, Foster loved to lawn bowl, and both he and my mother were active in the church.

A young family from their church bought the Perry Court home. It was recently listed on a historical tour in Wauwatosa. I was able to take this tour and it brought back numerous memories: the clothes chute from the top floor to the laundry in the basement, the shale tile hall, the wooden floors. But the rosemaling, a traditional Norwegian form of decorative painting on wood, was gone from the kitchen walls.

Just before Thanksgiving, 1998, the nursing home called and said Foster died of a heart attack, age ninety-four, in Mynnette's arms. Before this, he had decided he wanted some of his ashes buried with his birth father and mother in Illinois, and some with his wife, Mynnette, in her family plot in Iowa.

After his cremation, Mynnette Jean (M.J.) and I took some of his ashes to the Lanark, Illinois cemetery, where the groundskeeper was mowing the cemetery lawn. We each used a brand-new trowel to dig a shallow hole. M.J. had borrowed (stolen?) a Gideon Bible from the motel we were staying in, and she read a bit of scripture from it; we sang "Amazing Grace," placed his ashes in the hole and replaced the sod. The cemetery headstones of the Sheller plot were very interesting to us, because we found the names of our relatives.

Are you there gin? It's me, Mary Ann at 80.

We wondered, because of the shallow hole we dug for part of our father's ashes, if parts of Foster were spread afar by the mower man cutting the grass around where those ashes were buried.

I think my father gave all of us a wonderful example of how to succeed in life, despite his tough upbringing, the Depression and how difficult his marriage might have been at times. He was persistent, and undaunted by circumstance: a hard-worker, go-getter, and a winner! And I loved him very much.

CHAPTER 4

Childhood Memories- The Good, The Bad and The Ugly

*The best thing about the good old days
was that I wasn't good, and I wasn't old.
~ Seen on T-shirt*

DATELINE: WAUWATOSA, WISCONSIN

In kindergarten, I bit Jimmy S. in the stomach. He was riding the only kiddie car and I knew it was my turn to have it. When he did not give the kiddie car to me, I went bonkers and bit him. I'm not sure if I drew blood. As punishment, I was left seated in the nursing station for what seemed to me like a mournfully long time.

In 1st grade, Jojo L. kissed me in front of the class, and I thought I would die. Do you remember your first kiss? Mine was NOT like the movie kisses.

We put on a play for our parents. I was "Cora Carrot." My lines were, "Wake up vegetables, wake up fruits, wake up, wakeup." I have no idea why I remember this now, when half the time I go into a room in our condo and I can't remember why I went there.

At recess, we would always play "boys chase the girls." When the girls were caught, we would be placed in "jail." The jail was the backdrop for the baseball pitch. Do you think this exemplifies an early female/male role reversal?

Many times, after school, a few of the boys would chase me home and this terrified me, as I had to climb up a hill before I got home. And I wasn't a fast runner. I had no idea what they would do to me if they caught me and why in the heck didn't they catch me? As I approached the hill, I would start shouting for my dog and if Laddie was out, he would come racing to me to scare the boys away (this is what I hoped for).

A few years later, Carlton, a boy across the street from where I lived, and I were working on his treehouse, in a tree in his yard. He was pounding with the hammer and wouldn't share the hammer with me. I finally grabbed it and hit him on the head a few times. I'm surprised he didn't push me out of the tree/maybe he was unconscious? We never played together after that.

My violent temper was not restricted to young male friends but also erupted with my older sister, M.J.

As a young child, my older sister and I had little to do with each other because of our six-year age difference. But we would often fight. During one of our worst fights, she locked herself in the downstairs bathroom. I grabbed a glass ashtray and pounded on the door with it, leaving a couple of dents in the wooden door. I don't remember how I was punished, but seeing the house forty years later, the door had been replaced by the new owners.

From my earliest memories, my sister and I always had a list of chores to do every Saturday morning. We couldn't leave the house to play with our friends until our chores were done (we played totally unsupervised in those good ole days). We had to dust the furniture/dust the stairs/sweep the hall/fill the bird bath/and change the bed sheets.

In grade school, the boys in our classes outnumbered the girls, sixteen to eight. There were several boys from the nearby Catholic orphanage in our classes. One of the boys had webbed feet, which totally fascinated me. I always wondered if he could swim faster. I never found out.

Speaking of feet, Claire and I would often wash the dishes in my kitchen with our bare feet! Why on earth my mother would let us do this is beyond me. We would sit on the edge of the sink (pre-dishwasher days) and wash everything but the sharp knives, with our toes. This image of us washing the dishes with our feet, reminds me of what monkeys do!

Actually, when my parents did get a dishwasher, I insisted the gold band Limoges china could safely go into the dishwasher. Well, pity, pity: now much of the gold band is off the china, polluting the ocean! I'm amazed my mother didn't kill me. I inherited this set of china and now, of course, I wash the china by hand.

Are you there gin? It's me, Mary Ann at 80.

Claire and I were "first and fast friends." We met when we were three years old. We both lived on Kavanaugh Place in Wauwatosa. We've known each other seventy-seven years. She describes me, when I was a child, as wearing my blond hair in braids, being poor in sports, having big blue eyes, skinny calves, and being a loyal friend but dishing out the dirt when necessary.

As young children, we were walking to my home in the winter and decided to "check out the ice" on the Honey Creek Parkway river. Claire fell in and got her snowsuit wet. She knew her mother would be mad about this, so we continued to my house. We didn't have a clothes dryer in those days, but my mother said she would take care of Claire's snowsuit. She hung Claire's snow pants in our laundry room and called Claire's mother, Tecla. Her phone number was Bluemound 8-2160! Mine was Greenfield 6-1289. And these were party lines, where if someone else was talking on the phone, you were supposed to hang up, but I didn't. I quietly listened to them talking. Lordy, lordy, how am I still able to remember this but not where I put my glasses this morning?

In the winter, there was a huge hill close to our home. One year, I had a new sled. I was coasting down the hill and at the bottom of the hill there were several giant trees, where you turned your sled to the left to coast between them. Well, I coasted into one of the trees and passed out. When I came to, there was an adult couple who said they would take me home, but I knew I shouldn't take a ride with strangers. I can't remember how they finally convinced me to get in their car and kindly took me home.

The black and white collie next door, Pam, was a lovely dog. In the winter Pam would come and try to help me walk through the deep Wisconsin snow by putting his mouth on my boot and dragging my foot forward. It initially scared me, but he never bit me. Dogs are wonderful.

Pam lived with Dale and Margaret S. They had two gay sons and a daughter, Debbie, who had Downs Syndrome. The S's were Christian Scientists and to have 3 children in the 1940's-50's who didn't fit the social pattern must have been difficult for them.

Debbie attended a residential school in Pennsylvania. She would come home on vacations. I remember walking with her to my elementary school playground and some nasty children teasing her. I'm surprised I didn't bite them!

It must have been extremely hard for both the sons to cope with their sexuality and society particularly when they were both in mandatory military service.

Fred, the younger one, went to Yale and I remember him singing to me in our kitchen, "A room full of pearls" and giving me a necklace of pearls. Fred was much taller than me and I was totally smitten. Fred wore a crew cut and I wanted to run my hand over his hair. He let me.

Dale was in the Navy. One night when he was home on leave, he was sleepwalking and went out onto their roof in the rain. His father heard this and carefully got him back into their home. The thought of this really scared me.

One time, the S's went on a holiday and they left their car keys with my parents. My parents went out one night and my sister was babysitting me. She said we should take their car and go to the drive-in. She was at least sixteen as she was driving, so I was

Are you there gin? It's me, Mary Ann at 80.

probably around ten. We went to see *Scaramouche*, but we did not stay to the end of the movie as we began to get scared about being caught by our parents.

When we got back to our *cul- de-sac*, our parents were home. My sister turned off the car lights and we silently coasted down the hill into the S's driveway. Then we nonchalantly walked into our house. Both parents looked furious. Mother told me to go upstairs to bed. I don't remember what punishment my sister was dealt, but it was obviously worse than me going to bed.

In 4th grade, Dorothy V. and I got our class to stay outside on the playground after the noon bell rang, as our teacher had previously shortened our recess time and I didn't think this was fair. The two worst behaved boys in our class did not stay outside but went in at the bell. We could see our teacher and the principal pacing up and down the hall. When we finally went in, our teacher asked the class to write down if we were responsible for staying outside, and of course I admitted it. So, Dorothy and I had to stay after school several days and write some stupid sentence one thousand times. I knew I wouldn't have to serve my whole sentence as my family was going to visit my grandparents in Florida very soon. Dorothy was also reprieved after I left for Florida.

In 6th grade we had a wonderful teacher, Miss E. But after Christmas, she transferred to a different school to be a librarian. I was crushed and I just hated the next teacher, whose name I've repressed. During most of her math classes, I just looked out the window and did not pay attention. When I think of this now, I was probably depressed about our wonderful teacher leaving and in turn, I hated math and the new teacher.

While in elementary school, every Wednesday afternoon we got out of school to go to Bible School at the church of our choice. Most children went to the Congregational Church. Some were Methodist, Lutheran or Presbyterian and a few were Catholic. There was one Jewish girl in our Brownie troop. She invited our troop to her home and showed us special dishes her family used on religious holidays. I was quite impressed by her family having all these dishes.

At Christmas time, our church children's choir went to the public orphanage and sang carols to the children. I really hated doing this, as our parents brought us to the orphanage all dressed up and the children in the orphanage had to sit there and listen to and look at us.

One Sunday, Ann S. and I had been to Sunday school and we had an hour to kill while our parents were at the main service. We found this little door above the sanctuary, with a wooden plank inside, and started running up and down the plank. Suddenly, Mrs. L., Dr. Reverend L's ugly wife with frizzy gray hair, beady black eyes, and pinched facial features, yanked the door open and dragged us out. We didn't know below us the chandeliers were swinging back and forth and Dr. L. thought the end of the world was coming and started preaching hell, fire, and brimstone, while many of the congregation started to run outside of the sanctuary.

On Sundays, my father would often go downtown and bring home a sailor to share our family chicken dinner. My sister said the sailors were from the Great Lakes Naval Station. I have no idea how each sailor was selected. These dinners were always uncomfortable for me as everyone was so stilted.

On the weekend, I remember we often went to the Farmers' Market in West Allis to get fresh food. One time my father brought home a live chicken and wrung its neck in the backyard. I nearly threw up and I remember not wanting to eat that chicken.

In 6th grade, several of my friends and I went to Children's Theatre plays at the high school on Saturday afternoons. On the way there, we would stop at a little store in Wauwatosa village to get a candy bar or sweets. I rarely had any money, so I stole what I needed. I also stole from the Dime Store. My conscience caught up with me eventually and I told my mother. She made me try to figure out

Are you there gin? It's me, Mary Ann at 80.

the cost of what I stole from the Dime Store and take this amount back to the manager. I did not tell her about my candy store theft.

I am and I was dreadful with numbers - remember my 6th grade math class? So, the money estimate I gave my mother was probably exceedingly low. The Dime Store manager told me to never come back into his store. The following week, I did return to the Dime Store and I stole something else, to test him. Just to let you know, while in junior high school, my thieving permanently stopped.

Junior high school was 7th, 8th and 9th grade. My parents got one of the first T.V.'s and I had my school homeroom come to our house to watch something on the fuzzy T.V. screen. I think it was about an A bomb going off.

Many of us in junior high school took dancing lessons from Mrs. D. The girls would sit on one side of the room and the boys would sit on the other side. Then the boys would come and ask the girls to dance. There were usually more girls than boys, so the remaining girls would have to dance with each other. I did NOT like this.

I played the violin with the junior high school orchestra. I was also taking piano and drum lessons. At our first orchestra concert, my parents were sitting in the front row. I was sitting in the last chair of the second violins. Just before the concert started, the G string on my violin broke and I yelled, "My G-string broke." Mr. R., the conductor, glared at me and sent me to the music room. As I was passing my parents, my father was laughing his head off and I couldn't understand why. I didn't forget this incident and I finally "I got it" when I was in college!

In 8th grade, Lois R. and I were sneaking into the school (Lord knows why) and we got caught by the horrid, fat principal. He chased us around and around swinging doors and finally called our parents. My mother didn't let me go to the upcoming dance, which was probably just as well as I wasn't popular, and I bet no one would have asked me to dance.

In 9th grade, my homeroom and history teacher, Mr. L., told us to study our lesson, as he had an errand to do. After he left the room, I got the whole class to try and put their arm around the back of their head and touch their other ear. Having very few muscles, I could do this. When he came back into the room, we were all attempting this. He made me stay after school every day for a week, with my arm in this position for ½ hour! At some point during this year, my mother asked Mr. L. over for dinner at our house. I have no understanding of why she did this and I had to make baked Alaska for dessert. Perhaps I was flunking history?

My sister told me our mother had him over too, when she was in junior high. Maybe our mother had a liking for Mr. L.?

My parents sent me to summer camp for at least one to four weeks, to give them a break from parenting. I liked going to camp and have many pleasant memories of things I did and things I learned. I stopped going to camp each summer when I was in high school.

In 9th grade, the girls took Home Economics (Home Ec) and the boys took some course about making things. I did not like Home Ec. A few of us also considered ourselves much smarter than our instructor, Miss S. So, to get out of class, I invented the word "zorch" and told Miss S. I was not feeling well and was having a "zorch" attack. She excused me from class. She probably thought "zorch" meant I was having my period or cramps. I hadn't even started to menstruate yet, but she didn't know that.

We also had to take some science course, which I hated. Not only the subject matter but the teacher. At one point, when our teacher was out of the room, I got the rows of students to rock their chairs in a rhythm…first row forward, second row back, third row forward, fourth row back. When our teacher came into the room, we started our chairs moving. I don't know how he stopped us from doing this, but it gave me great pleasure and humor to do this. And thinking about it now, our regulated oscillation may have been some scientific principal. I wonder if he lost a "teaching moment" or I did?

One of the Girl Scout camps I went to had a goat. But the goat had to be taken care of before camp, so the goat came to stay in our yard for a few days. My dog, Laddie, was in heaven. At last he had something to do. He would chase the goat around, jump up on the picnic table and bark at the goat. Then the goat got on the picnic table and bunted Laddie off the table.

One Sunday, I put the goat on a leash and walked it a few miles to the church. The children's Sunday School class LOVED it and what they loved most was the goat defecating in front of them. I don't remember what happened after that for me or the goat, but I walked it back to our yard.

One camp I loved was in Muskegon, Michigan: Camp Minnewanka. I always felt seasick on the ferry ride across Lake Michigan, to and from camp. I went there for three years and after my camp session, I worked in the camp kitchen for two of those years, giving my parents even more of a break. I was dating one of the "locals" and he wanted to marry me, but I said no to proposal #1. He came to Wauwatosa to see me, in hopes I had changed my mind, but I hadn't.

Going to high school was exciting. A group of us walked to and from school as we were still too young to drive and none of us could afford to pay for a car. I would leave around 7:30 a.m., as we had sports before and after classes and I wanted to get away from my mother, who I hated (a teenage developmental stage of mine).

I had braces put on my teeth my freshman year and it was very painful when kissing. I dated a little bit but no one "sent me over the moon." I took Latin and Spanish. My Latin teacher made each student stand if they didn't know the answer to her questions, so I feel like I stood through 2 years of Latin. I loved my English classes, including writing poetry and fortunately, one of my poems was published in a poetry softcover book. English was my favorite subject. I was surprised and thrilled when my poem was accepted.

My sister got married in 1955, when I was a sophomore in high school; and it was quite the event. I had joined a high school club called Red Arrow. You take a pledge you won't drink or smoke when you are initiated into the club, and you are required to compete in various sports, get top marks and do many hours of community work.

Well, at her wedding reception, I had a teeny glass of champagne. The guilt I felt was overwhelming. So, the next week, I went to our club/teacher and confessed. I was barely forgiven. The only

Are you there gin? It's me, Mary Ann at 80.

reason I got my athletic credits was because Claire was my doubles badminton partner and she was/is a whiz.

I was playing competitive piano duets with another young woman. We were enrolled in a big competition coming up. My mother said if I didn't have a B grade point average, I could not be in the competition. Well, you know the story. I had to drop out of the competition, and I was so mad at my mother, I stopped taking piano lessons. A typical teenager response.

During that year, my parents went on a holiday without me. An older lady, who use to help my mother with cleaning and entertaining, came to stay with me. Laddie was not feeling well and had been sick during the day. I couldn't take him to the vet as I was not driving yet, and I had to check coats at a football game in the evening, so I let Laddie outside. He never came back. I think he probably went into the woods behind our house and died. I was beside myself with guilt and loss. Ted G., a good friend, came over and we walked all over the woods looking for Laddie, but we never found him. It still saddens me to remember the loss of my beloved, loyal pet I had for over seven years. OO! So terribly sad.

Junior year, my homeroom nominated me for Junior Prom Queen. Fortunately, I came in second and I only got to ride on the float. I wasn't dating anyone special and it would have been hard for me to find a Junior Prom King if I won.

Roger F. was my "first love." Part way through my junior year, he asked me out. He was a year ahead of me in high school and when he asked me out, I was thrilled and floored. He taught me to drive a stick shift car, his car, a truly trusting friend. He went to Wisconsin University the next year, joined a fraternity and wanted me to join him for parties in Madison. I didn't think I could go as I was 1) in Red Arrow, 2) I was sure my parents would not let me go and 3) I was scared to be with these older people, who drank, 4) I had no idea where would I stay, and 5) did I have enough money to pay for this?

That year, at Christmas, when he was home, he asked me to marry him, proposal #2! I told him I needed to go to college for four years, would he wait? I knew my parents would NOT pay for any wedding of mine at age seventeen. No, he would not wait for me, he had a girlfriend in Madison! I was totally crushed. And I vowed I would never, ever "fall" for another male. Roger married this woman; he eventually became the richest man in Wisconsin (!) and died of Lou Gehrig's disease when he was in his seventies. If I had married him, I would have had to become Lutheran.

The summer between my junior and senior year in high school, I set up a program at the nearby Wisconsin Veterans Hospital. For some reason, I heard these men NEVER got to go outside as there was not enough staff. So, I organized several Red Arrow friends to go every Saturday for a couple of hours and take the vet they had been paired with, outside. The first day, the man in the wheelchair I took outside started crying. I didn't say anything as I wasn't sure what to say. Finally, he blew his nose and told me this was the first time, in over 10-15 years he had been able to touch grass, see a squirrel hopping around and feel the fresh air. This made me want to cry. The men we took outside wanted a picture of each of us teenagers, which was fine. At the end of the summer, it was sad to say "goodbye" to each of these vets, as we weren't sure another group would be there the following summer.

My senior year in high school was very busy, applying for college, keeping my grades up, being very active in Red Arrow and in sports. Even though I wasn't good in sports, I loved participating. We had a great female marching group that performed at football games… or was it basketball games?

In 1957, the Wauwatosa High School female volleyball team won the Milwaukee, Wisconsin Championships and I saved the little statue we each received. I gave this statue to my younger granddaughter as she is getting involved with volleyball. I could barely

Are you there gin? It's me, Mary Ann at 80.

get the ball over the net on my serves, I certainly couldn't strike it down onto our opponent's side, but I did make a lot of cheering noise for our team. Then, at our Red Arrow awards night, I won another little statue for being the most supportive person or something like that.

Remembering these events from my childhood is delightful: seeing how I perceived things then and now. Recording these memories gives me a great deal of pleasure. "Memories, look a new day has begun."

CHAPTER 5

College and Early Work History

If I say I will do it, I will do it!
No need to reminding me every 6 months.
~ Seen on T-shirt

IN SEPTEMBER 1957, MY parents drove me to the Chicago train station and put me on a train to Syracuse, N.Y. with my trunkload of stuff. A bus driver would meet me in Syracuse and take me to Wells College, in Aurora, N.Y. I was quite excited about this new adventure.

There was a very handsome young man in the same train car. After a while, he came over and introduced himself. He went to a nearby men's college and said he would see me in the fall when we had college mixers. And we did date a little, but I didn't know how to jitterbug, so he dropped me.

My freshman year at Wells was wonderful and I learned to jitterbug. My roommate, Marion, was/is a gem. Because her name is Marion and mine is Mary Ann, our floor decided one of us needed to have a nickname. Marion was thin, very active and someone

Are you there gin? It's me, Mary Ann at 80.

suggested she was "like a cricket." So, to this day, she is called Cricket! She is also a P.E.O. which was a great surprise to both of us when we found this out as we went to our 40th Wells' reunion.

A now defunct tradition at Wells was for the junior class to pick the five "prettiest" freshmen to stand at the five points of the W during their junior prom march. My sister was picked during her freshman year. When my name was called in 1957, I couldn't believe it. I didn't think I was attractive at all. Cricket and I were sitting on an antique table during this whole event and the table broke. Her parents and mine were sent the repair bill. My mother never told me what it cost them.

Saturday night at Wells was steak night. Many times, one of us had a date come to dinner. Before we started eating, I would say, "eat to the left" and we would all start eating from the plate to our left, so the poor starving young man would have to eat from some skimpy plate on his left while the woman to his right was eating from his pile of food.

I think the best summer job I had during my college years, was working at the C Lazy U Ranch in Granby, Colorado, as a chambermaid. Cleaning rooms gave me a direct education regarding contraception!

Some of the workers and I attended a concert Harry Belafonte was giving in the nearby open-air Red Rocks Amphitheatre. I will never forget him coming onto the stage in a glowing maroon shirt, and his wonderful voice.

I received my 3rd marriage proposal at this ranch. David, one of the summer workers, was going to Harvard to study law in the fall. His divorced father was a lawyer and I can't remember what his mother did, I think she was a physician. They lived in Kansas. We both went back to our colleges after a torrid summer.

At Christmas, he sent a puppy to me in Wauwatosa. The poor little dog cried all night, drove my mother mad, and she finally called

David's mother and told her that "WE" were sending the dog back as I was in college in New York State and she didn't want to train it.

David and I were engaged, and he came to Aurora, N.Y. to see me, and Sally, who had worked at the ranch and lived nearby in Rochester, NY. Sally probably had somewhat of a relationship with him at the ranch, even though they were not engaged. After David left, I told him I didn't want to marry him, and he asked me to send the ring back. Not a big deal. Actually, it was a big deal, as I was very poor, and I had to insure this ring.

As a freshman at Wells, I got "fixed up" with Harry. He was in graduate school at Cornell, having served in the military before this. I couldn't imagine what he would see in me with our age differences. We had an off-again, on-again relationship. After I graduated, I met him at his parent's home in Ohio. His mother DID NOT LIKE ME. I sensed it immediately. Harry had previously driven to Wauwatosa to see where I lived and never contacted me or my parents! Is this sick? At any rate, he proposed to me (#4) but I did not accept this as I was "dating Jack and others." Harry married someone else, but kept in touch with me for many, many years.

After my second husband, Ian, and I married, I e-mailed Harry because he cycled. He gave me much information about bikes, training etc. and he often sent me small gifts with my name on them. He painted a great picture of our home on 27th Avenue, which Ian and I hung in the hall.

Harry played the banjo with a Dixieland band in every community he lived in. When he and his wife were in Sun City, AZ (where the Shellers had lived, and Harry looked up their home/activities …still a bit of a sicko), he sent me a recording of the band he played with in AZ. I was thrilled to get it, as I was into housework that day and not thrilled with the routine tasks. Listening to the music while I cleaned, made the housework MUCH easier.

Are you there gin? It's me, Mary Ann at 80.

I called Harry to thank him and his response totally turned me off...he had to go into another room so his wife (who is/was a P.E.O.) would not hear him talking to me! At that point, I realized I was being victimized/stalked in an insidious, creepy way. I e-mailed him I was destroying his painting. I was giving all the athletic clothing he gave me to the Goodwill and not to EVER contact me again. When I trashed the painting, he had written under the back paper I was his one and only love. Thank heavens I didn't marry him! I felt totally sorry for the woman he did marry.

Three summers during high school and college, I worked at the Sanitarium (the so-called nut house) in Wauwatosa. The first summer I was put to work on the "worst" ward, so I would not be afraid of these people. These people needed to have their closet doors locked so they wouldn't try suicide.

I was locking one large woman's closet door and she told me she had permission to keep it open. I kept locking the door and turned to leave her room when she grabbed me by the throat and started squeezing. Fortunately, a nurse was walking by and threw her weight against the hall door, nudging the patient. This patient had been given permission for her closet door to be open, but I had not read her chart before I started working. I apologized to her and she acted as if she hadn't heard me. I think her psychiatrist probably upped her drug load because of her response to my behavior, but I don't know. I felt terrible about not "doing my job correctly."

Another summer at the Sanitarium, I just needed to keep the drugs away from the patients during the night. So, I sat up all night, with the drug box on my lap. I watched T.V. until midnight, when it stopped, then I did my homework and read books. That summer, I needed to go to summer school to make up for a course I had flunked at Wells (Personal and Family Finance!). After my ethics course at Marquette University and my workload, I would come home at 7 a.m. and go to sleep until noon, get up, go to school, etc.

Okay, we're back to early history. The first Thanksgiving at college, I couldn't afford to go home, so Cricket invited me to her home in Hopewell Junction, New York. Her home was lovely, on huge acreage. And her mother used the same Haviland Limoges gold band china my mother had.

Cricket's mother had her Matinee Musical ladies over for tea while we were there. She asked Cricket and me to sing a few songs for them.

This is the first song we sang:

"Sam's chick Minnie had lots of style,

When he breathes deeply, it makes her smile.

She's closer to him than the hair on his chest,

She'll never leave him flat,

For what Sam paid, he got the best,

She is a tattoo painted on his chest."

We finished with:

"We like great big, hairy chested men,

Hairy chested men,

We like great big, hairy chested men,

We are the sweet Wells girls."

We thought we were hilarious, the ladies didn't.

Jeffie, Cricket's brother, took me for a ride on the tractor, as he was mowing the grass. I pulled a rusty cotter pin on the tractor that went through the base of his boot into his foot. Being a Christian

Are you there gin? It's me, Mary Ann at 80.

Science family, I knew Jeffie hadn't had a tetanus shot and I was terrified his foot would have to be amputated. I washed it as best I could; they called a "practitioner" who came twice. I saw Jeffie again at Christmas and there was absolutely NO scar on his foot. Miracle #1.

During my sophomore year at Wells, I suggested a few of us hide in the laundry truck in dirty laundry bins to escape Wells (even though we "signed out" in our dorms.) The laundry truck went back to Ithaca, where Cornell University is. Carol, Sue and I hid in three bins of dirty sheets until we were well outside of Aurora, N.Y. When we popped up, I was surprised the truck driver didn't go into the ditch. As we approached a hotel, where he needed to get more dirty laundry, he suggested we go in for a drink. We did not take his offer. When we were in Ithaca, he dropped us off, far away from the laundry. I do not remember how we got back to Wells.

On a bicycle adventure at Wells, I suggested three of us, Carol, Margie and me, ride our bikes to Cornell on a Sunday, thirty miles away. Our bikes did not have gears. We left Wells early, but the few restaurants in route were closed, as it was Sunday. We saw a farm; we went up to the door and asked if the wife would make us breakfast, telling her our plight. She was WONDERFUL. We had a full breakfast and left what we thought was the amount of money for the food. At one point, her husband thundered in, then went out.

Unfortunately, it was parent's weekend at Cornell, so our "possible" rides back to Wells were non-existent. I was dating Harry and I thought he might be able to give us a ride back to Wells, which he did, sans bicycles.

The (notice how I've said the, not my) next serious boyfriend was Tom. He was a year ahead of me at Cornell, majoring in entomology. We went together, then not together, then together. His best friend, Peter, I introduced to a Wells classmate of mine and they really hit it off. Unfortunately, Tom and Peter were into heavy drugs after university. Peter and my friend divorced several years after they married. I have no idea what happened to Tom. His parents were caring, kind people.

During the summer between my junior and senior year, another Milwaukee student at Wells, Barbara, asked if I would drive her car back to Wells as she was flying to NYC to see her boyfriend. I was happy to do this, and I got two Wells students from Chicago to travel with me. We decided we would drive through the night as it was too expensive to stay at a motel. We stopped around 4 a.m. at an all-night café for some eggs and coffee.

There were three young men there and the six of us started talking and laughing. They went to college fairly close to us and had been to another girls' college mixer. We decided we would see who could get to Niagara Falls first and whoever got there last would have to buy the other three a meal. When our car got to the Niagara Falls turn off, I just kept driving on to Wells.

The following weekend, Barbara drove her car into NYC to see her boyfriend. On her way, she said another car kept honking at her, flashing their lights, cutting in front of her. She finally stopped on the turnpike. They pulled up next to her and asked her if she knew someone named Mary Ann Sheller.

She told me later, they were furious with me as they waited about 45 minutes for us at Niagara Falls, and were worried we had been in an accident.

Cricket and I roomed together all four years in college. Our 4th year, we asked Holly to join us.

Cricket had a very sore tooth our senior year in college. I insisted she go to see a dentist in a nearby town. She said she would go see a dentist but was going to stop and see a practitioner first. She was back in no time at all. She said he read to her and the toothache went away. I checked the inside of her mouth. There was no discoloration or swelling that had been there when she left. Miracle #2.

I think I was depressed for a time at Wells. I am not sure why. My mother had her first major cancer operation when I was a fresh-

Are you there gin? It's me, Mary Ann at 80.

man. I wound up in the Wells infirmary around that time, probably trying to cope with the possible loss of my mother. My folks were going on a vacation, a year or so later, and I managed to go back to 1083 during this time. I found great comfort from Margaret, our Christian Science neighbor. But I still had to complete my courses and graduate from Wells.

I graduated from Wells in 1961. M.J. and our parents came to my graduation. M.J. was there when the senior parade to commencement started, but my parents weren't. I asked M.J. why our parents weren't there and she said because they were probably "doing it." I couldn't believe old people still "did it."

After graduation, I moved to NYC with two classmates.

CHAPTER 6

Pre-Marriage History

*Does running from my responsibilities
count as cardio?
~ Seen on T-shirt*

THE SUMMER OF 1961, I moved into New York City with Jeannie and Holly. We had this teeny, 3rd floor, one-bedroom apartment on 64th street, between Lexington and Park Avenue. Whoever came in last, slept on the couch in our living room.

Jeannie had a convertible car. As we were unloading her car with our stuff, robbers were taking our stuff out the third-floor attic window! They didn't take much before we realized what was happening. We called the police and they just laughed!

When we were in college, Cricket went to Japan one summer on a U.S. foreign exchange program. Our doorbell in N.Y.C. rang. I was the only one home, so I went downstairs to see who it was. It was a strange young man who said something that sounded like Cricket's name, so I invited him in and gave him a glass of orange juice. He gave me the creeps. Our phone rang and it was a call for me. I told the woman not to hang up if she heard me scream, as there was a visitor in our apartment I was going to ask to leave. I

Are you there gin? It's me, Mary Ann at 80.

took his empty glass and opened our door and he reluctantly left. I thanked my friend on the phone. Later, I looked out our window and he was across the street, staring up at our apartment. When my roommates came home, I told them about this and there he was, staring up at our apartment. However, whenever we left, we never saw him. This went on for about a week.

One summer night, the three of us decided to go to an outdoor theatre to hear Joan Sutherland sing. She made her debut at Wells the year before this, singing in the Wells gym!

We piled into Jeannie's convertible with the top down, all dressed up, driving through rough neighborhoods without a care in the world! Joan was absolutely gorgeous, floating onto the stage and filling the summer air with her beautiful voice. We put the top up on the way home. And fortunately, the three of us arrived at our apartment safely.

Another neat thing we did in NYC, was go to the opening of the Lincoln Center by limo. I think Jeannie's fiancé, Dave, arranged for the four of us to ride in the limo.

I had a job in the executive training program of Bloomingdales Department Store. It was a fun job, lots of interesting people, like Paul Newman and Joanne Woodward attended our shop. In fact, Fred, my pearl giver, came looking for me!

We were now the same height and really had nothing to talk about other than it was nice seeing him again. My mother probably still communicated with his mother.

And I remember one time, Holly's older brother, Norm, took me to Bloomingdales on his motor scooter, with me wearing my Nina Ricci hat, sitting sidesaddle behind him.

At Christmas time, Bloomingdales staff asked me to help run the Antique Gift Shop, beside a young graduate from Harvard named Dick. Dick was very funny, easy to work with and smart. We had one date, but there were no sparks between us. Only later did I realize he was the son of the Texas high-end Neiman and Marcus Department Store owners!

Holly, Jeannie and I moved out of this apartment into an apartment on 79th street, above Chardas Restaurant, where we could never afford to eat. Our next move was to an apartment on the west side close to the Museum of Natural History. We finally moved into an apartment near the theatre district, close to where *West Side Story* was filmed. My parents would not get out of their car to see our apartment when they came to visit!

I started taking courses at NYU working towards my master's degree in psychology.

Holly introduced me to Jack, in New York City. He was tons of fun, in the service, flying airplanes. Jack's family lived in a very prestigious area of Philadelphia, but he was Catholic, and my parents would have had a fit if we married.

At one point, I was going to visit M. J. and Jim in Ohio. Harry drove me to their home after I had met his parents, and rejected his marriage offer. Harry was a tenacious sort. I stayed with M.J. and Jim for a few days. Jack arrived, on his way back from Texas and drove me to his home in Philadelphia!

Jack, a friend of his, Mike, also in the service, and Colleen, who I was working with at Bloomingdales, went to Nassau for a week at Christmas, as Mike and Jack were now stationed in the Caribbean.

When it was time for Jack and Mike to return to their base, I suggested we get motor scooters to take them to the airport. If they could fly planes, they could certainly drive scooters. Jack said yes, the other two took a taxi with their luggage. I figured Colleen and I would tootle around the parking lot at the airport with our scooter to learn how to get the scooter back to the rental place.

Well, as Jack and I were zipping along, one of our tires hit gravel. Jack told me to hold on and I said, "No, it's free fall." That's the last thing I remember until I "came to" in a hospital room in Miami, Florida. (see Mary Ann's Health Chapter.)

Are you there gin? It's me, Mary Ann at 80.

One of my Wells friends fixed me up with a musician fellow from some foreign country. I remember on our second date, it was raining, we had no money and were walking back to my apartment on the west side of town. We started laughing and singing and then after we stopped singing, he asked me to marry him!!! (#5)

I quit my job at Bloomingdales, as it was totally too stressful for me. I got a job with the NYU Medical Services, finding people who had had huge doses of x-ray as children to clean up their ringworm. The question was, did the large amount of x-ray cause cancer? There were five of us working on this. Doreen was a beautiful black woman, the nurse was a single, ugly Catholic, the other 2 women were Jewish. Doreen invited me to her wedding, which was going to be in New Jersey. After her honeymoon, she asked me why I didn't come to her wedding. I told her I didn't want to stand out. She looked at me and said, "What makes you think you were the only white person invited?" Touché.

Martha, a friend from Wells, fixed me up with my first husband. He was working on his master's degree at Columbia University and working at an insurance company. We were the same religion, his family was very gentle, we liked many of the same things, so when he asked me to marry him (#6), I said yes. We were married in a New York City church.

CHAPTER 7

Seven Year Marriage History with First Husband

*My first husband thought I was crazy
but I'm not the one who married me.
~ Seen on T-shirt*

MY PARENTS WERE CIVIL to him but didn't like him. My sister couldn't come to our wedding as one of her girls had chickenpox. Holly and Cricket (who was now married) were my maids of honor. Martha was angry with me, because since she had introduced me to my husband, I should have included her in the wedding party. I didn't know this was the protocol.

Earlier in the week, I bumped into Mary, a friend from junior high school, who was working as a nurse in NYC. She married a son of the conductor who threw me out of my first concert in junior high school. I invited her to my wedding, and she said she would come but she would be in uniform. I said that was just fine.

Are you there gin? It's me, Mary Ann at 80.

It reminded me of a time I worked at the Sanitarium in Wauwatosa, when one of the patients wanted to go to the Catholic Church and I had to accompany her, dressed in my white uniform, walking through the Wauwatosa main area, including across railroad tracks. I worried she might try to run away, and I wondered if I could run fast enough to catch her.

My first husband and I went camping on our honeymoon in a southeastern state park. What we didn't know was the Boy Scouts of America County Representatives were camping in the same park. So, between bugles and prying eyes, we left the park soon after we arrived.

At one of the other parks we visited, we missed the closing time and we were locked in. My husband went to a run-down house to see if he could make a phone call, but they didn't have a phone. They pointed to a sign saying where we could get a hold of a park ranger. Instead, my husband found two wide flat boards, placed them on the low park gate and, had me drive our sports car up the boards, then down the other side. Fortunately, I didn't swerve!

We got an apartment in East Orange, New Jersey, and commuted to work each day. We both continued taking university courses. I stopped working about two weeks before Holly was born. I remember the bus driver telling me if I went into labor on his bus, I was NOT to tell him!

When we first moved into the apartment, we didn't have a table, so we ate our meals at the piano with the cover over the keys. We turned our dining room into Holly's room.

I wanted to see my baby born and I asked my doctor to please put up a mirror. I was thinking of the kind of mirrors that are in dressing rooms in department stores. When he came into the delivery room, he had one of those teeny round things on the top of his head. I did not have my glasses on and obviously with my legs up and his head down, I saw nothing of my daughter's birth.

In 1963, most mothers used bottled milk for infants; nursing was out. Well, it wasn't out for me…I was determined to nurse. I thought I was doing it right until a nurse came in, grabbed my breast, and Holly's mouth and NURSING began.

Our bedroom window, which faced the fire escape, had bars over it. In the kitchen, there was an area that had once held a dumbwaiter. It was crawling with cockroaches. I think we threw our garbage down this opening. In the night, when I would get up to feed Holly, there would be scritching and scattering noises in the kitchen, no matter how much I cleaned the surfaces… YUCK.

In those days Pampers had not been invented, and even had they been, we would not have been able to afford them. Cloth diapers were in. We were very poor. But when I think of us being very poor, I remember that shortly before we were married, my first husband was able to go on a European skiing trip with my college friend, Holly. I couldn't afford it.

Prior to their trip, Holly gave me parakeet so I could teach it to talk before they left so I wouldn't be lonely. This didn't work. I hated the bird and hated my husband going to Europe to ski with my best friend. Somehow the bird died before their return.

I had one week of diaper service when Holly was born. Then I washed her diapers.

My mother came to help me and to see her new granddaughter.

She brought cigarettes from the plane! She and I smoked in our kitchen.

I remember being at my Wauwatosa home, with Grandma Lomas, mother, M.J., and myself (so I must have been 16), all smoking when our father and Daddy Frank walked in! Totally disgusting.

There was a diaper pail in our apartment bathroom. It leaked into the apartment below us. Again, totally disgusting. I don't think we were fined but we got another diaper pail.

Are you there gin? It's me, Mary Ann at 80.

My first husband and I talked about him getting his Ph.D. so he applied to various graduate schools.

In the meantime, I worked as a secretary for two kitchen gadget inventors. I got to help myself to each of their gadgets, so guess what family members got for Christmas! Teflon had just come onto the market and they told me if I could think of a kitchen gadget that would work with Teflon, I would get 1/3 of their proceeds. Unfortunately, I couldn't think of anything.

Besides my job, I was also taking courses to get my teaching degree.

A neighbor took care of Holly during the day and saw her take her first steps. I nearly cried when she told me this. I would have loved to witness this.

My husband was accepted into two graduate schools and chose the University of Minnesota. When we got there, I applied and got a job for two years teaching at a private kindergarten in a suburb, Bloomington, and later as director of a day activity center in Rosedale. I also started my master's program in psychology at the University.

We lived on the first floor of a duplex, very close to campus. We found a delightful woman to look after Holly while we were in school and working. She would play hide and seek with Holly and would climb into the bathtub and lie down. We wondered if she was sipping some of our liquor, but we were never quite sure. I think her name was Mrs. M.

The day activity center where I worked with children and young adults with mental challenges, was in a church. The very young children came in the morning and the young adults in the afternoon.

There was a small animal zoo in St. Paul. I borrowed a nanny goat and her kid so these children and young adults could see and pet them.

The goats rode well in the backseat of our car, with the nanny's head out the window, surprising many other drivers. The nanny ate just about everything in our garden, which ticked me off.

We had one car and a Vespa motor scooter. I would usually ride the latter to the school/church, as it was quite a distance and gas was cheaper to fuel this vehicle.

I remember one evening, there was a parent meeting at the school, I was wearing a white cotton dress and it started to rain on my way to the school, driving the Vespa. I was soaked. Fortunately, it was hot out and the dress dried rapidly.

In the late '60s there were all kinds of war protests going on, on campuses across the U.S. Holly was three to four years old and we were walking to the drug store. All of a sudden, I did not see where she was. She was NOT in the store, I ran onto the street and I did not see her, but I saw a police car. I went up to tell the officer she was missing and there she was, standing on the front seat of the police car. Holly remembers standing on the front seat of the police car looking for me through the front windshield; the police officer had driven her around to find me. Holly remembers seeing me and she said I was crying.

One night my husband and I went to see the movie, *Fahrenheit 451*. At the point when the books were being burned in the movie, there was a crashing noise in the theatre and the lights went out. Obviously, we all left as the front doors of the theatre were smashed and the power box was smashed because a tornado was tearing through Minneapolis. We charged home to find Holly safely in her bed and the babysitter taking refuge in the basement.

We had several dogs while we were in Minneapolis. One of the dogs was quite destructive. We would loosely tie him up in the kitchen, near his water and food when we went to school and work.

One day, I put a frozen piece of meat in a pot on the stove, knowing it would be defrosted by the time I got home from work. Well,

Are you there gin? It's me, Mary Ann at 80.

the dog smelled the meat and kept leaping at the stove, eventually turning on the burner under the pot and after a while setting the pot on the stove on fire. The students upstairs were home, called the fire department, who rescued the dog but not the meat. This dog's name was Barnie because he was born in a barn and smelled like a barn when we got him.

My favorite dog was Fudge. He was a puppy when we got him and we had him for several years, even after our move to Canada. He was very smart, and I remember testing him with some of my early psychological tests and he made it up to the three-year-old level; he was actually smarter than that, but he couldn't answer the verbal questions. At one point, he was in the house with a case of diarrhea and he tried to use both of our toilets.

When Holly was in 1st grade, I remember my first "parent" conference. The teacher said Holly was very smart, but she used foul language! I couldn't believe it as we did not swear. I asked the teacher to give me an example.

Well, it turned out, the teacher put the "smart" children next to the children who needed a bit of help. And before the parent conferences, the teacher had each child copy a letter to their parents from the blackboard and then told the children to write "love" and sign their names. The boy in front of Holly did not know how to spell love so he asked Holly to help him. She wrote, "fuck." He could not read this, but his parents certainly could!

It was all I could do not to laugh. We mentioned to Holly the only people who use words like that are those who aren't too bright, and Holly had enough words to erase this one from her vocabulary.

A few weeks later, we were having a dinner party and one of the guests said *damn* and Holly said, "Mother, I thought you and your friends didn't swear."

While in Minneapolis, Holly fell out of bed and broke her collar bone. Not a happy experience. Holly remembers lying in bed crying from the pain. I gave her an aspirin and told her to go to sleep.

She lay there and continued to cry until I came back and we went to the hospital.

Steve was born in July of 1969 when the first space rocket was launched for the moon. I came home with baby Steve, the night they landed on the moon. I remember burping him after feeding him. Fudge heard these sounds and came into the living room, put his head on my lap, and started making the same sounds. I think the dog missed me and was trying to get used to having another family member to love.

Dr. Spock was no longer "in" when Steve was born. So, when Steve peeped, I was there. When the public health nurse visited, she suggested I wait a bit and not jump with every noise he made.

Steve's crib and changing table were in the dining area, about 3 feet from our bedroom. Our bedroom was so small, we couldn't fall out of bed.

In Florida, my husband's mother had a heart attack and the doctor said he wouldn't let her out of the hospital until my husband's brother, Alan, found another place to live.

Alan had a neurological disorder and was in a wheelchair. Alan came to live with us. His bed was our living room couch. It was pretty tight quarters for all of us, including Fudge. Alan eventually attended a university fairly close by, until he went into a group home for the physically challenged.

Our marriage was not great, and we went for marriage counseling, which helped some. We would go out to eat after our sessions, have a martini, and a Reuben sandwich at The Lincoln Delicatessen.

We had many, many friends at the University. Often, they would wind up in our backyard and we would stretch the can of tuna fish by adding cup after cup of noodles.

We both finished our degrees. He could not find a job in the U.S. and knew there was a job opportunity at the University of British Columbia. He applied and was accepted. We moved to British Columbia, in the summer of 1970, with a U-Haul truck and our Volk-

Are you there gin? It's me, Mary Ann at 80.

swagen camper. Steve rode in a port-a-crib in the car and Holly sometimes sat with her father in the U-Haul.

On one part of our trip, we had to go under a low overpass. My husband let some of the air out of the U-Haul tires so the truck could move under the low overpass. Another time on this trip, we were driving late at night under a full moon and wild horses were charging alongside our vehicles. It was quite scary to see a horse's eye looking at you as you are speeding along.

Although my husband was working at the university, he wanted to live far away in Coquitlam as it was less expensive. We rented a house for the first couple of years, living next door to a fine family. Valinda and Holly became good friends. These people were wonderful neighbors. Valinda's father taught a course in high school.

The first year we were in BC, I did not work. Our house has never been so clean. I made two loaves of bread and gave one of them to Valinda to take to her family. Her mother never thanked me, and this was SO unlike them. I finally asked Valinda if the family liked the bread and she said, "Yes, my mother bakes 12 loaves a week." This was such a typically Canadian response. Betty probably felt terrible she hadn't given us a loaf of their bread.

Steve was very ill the first year we were in Coquitlam. A doctor put him in hospital in isolation and we had to suit up every time we went to see him. He didn't get any better in hospital and I finally had him discharged as I felt the doctor was not doing him any good.

We bought a house on Cove Place, with financial help from the Shellers, near the Ranch Park Elementary School.

I got a job teaching a special needs class at this school. It was challenging and interesting. One of the large, unruly boys won a ride home in my little sports car. When we got near his address, he wanted to get out. I didn't see his home, but I think he lived in a shack.

My class wasn't allowed to play on the playground during recess, so we would walk to my home and have a cup of hot chocolate. Fudge loved this as he got lots of attention. We had no furniture in our living room, and I remember hearing one of the boys say, "Isn't this wonderful, no teacher has ever had us to her home before."

At one point, the principal came into my classroom and wondered why it was so quiet. I showed him the behavior modification reward system I was using, and it was working.

My eldest niece, Lynne, and family were in Luxembourg. She was a teenager and dating an army guy in Luxembourg. He was transferred from Luxembourg to California. Lynne didn't want to lose her relationship with him so managed to get enough money to fly to New York City. My sister realized what was going on and had Lynne apprehended when the plane landed in New York City. She gave Lynne the choice of coming back to Luxembourg, living with her grandparents in Wauwatosa, or coming to live with us in Coquitlam. Obviously, she came to live with us.

I thought this would be great for her to live with us as she could "babysit" Holly and Steve. Not exactly. She connected with her army guy who had an apartment in Vancouver. We never met him. Lynne was able to connect with him during the day, but we said she needed to back at our home before 10 p.m.

At this same time, there was a rapist in Coquitlam. Lynne may have had a car ride with this dreadful person but was smart enough to get out of the car and hide from him while safely working her way back to our house.

In 1978, Fudge developed hip dysplasia, was getting old and I had him put to sleep. This was another tough one for all of us.

My husband was spending a good deal of time at the University, even on the weekends. When I called him, he would rarely answer

Are you there gin? It's me, Mary Ann at 80.

the phone. I wondered if he was having an affair, and he was! He left our home and got an apartment.

His girlfriend gave him a cat, which he brought back to our home when we tried again to make a go of our relationship. I developed an allergy to the cat! Are you laughing yet? After we decided to divorce, the place he found to live would not take cats! I found another home for his cat. And I began being a single parent after my husband got the seven-year itch.

CHAPTER 8

My Life as a Single Parent… Or Some of the More Interesting Parts of It

I thought growing old would take longer.
~ Seen on T-shirt

THE '70S WERE CERTAINLY a stressful time for me. My neighbor was very supportive of me. She and her husband were also divorced, and I remember one of the men I was dating told me he saw her husband in a bar with another woman. Dorothy told me one night she placed strings across the steps to their front door to trip Bart. It was the only time he came in their back entrance.

She called me to come over for a glass of wine after I had Fudge put to sleep. What a true friend. We cried together, even though Fudge had barked and barked, and this annoyed her. At the time, I had told her to spray him with her hose, but she never did and had never complained again.

Are you there gin? It's me, Mary Ann at 80.

Interesting single parent camping experiences:

1. Dorothy, her two children, me and my two children went on a camping trip. Madge, a friend of ours, was going to join us when she finished work. We got all set up at the camp and it started to rain. It wasn't raining hard, so we drove into the nearby town and called Madge to come anyhow, assuring her we would be there. Well, when we got back to our site, it started to pour. We packed up and went home. Madge got to the park and of course couldn't find us. She was then locked in the park all night. We are sure she helped herself to some of the alcoholic beverages she brought. Madge banged on both of our doors very early the next morning, still mad! After breakfast and coffee, things settled down and our friendship resumed.

2. My friend, Donna, Holly, Steve and I went camping next to a river outside of Squamish. We didn't have to pay to camp there and we took Fudge as our protector. No one else was camping there. Donna and I decided we would sleep outside on the bank next to the river. The children would sleep in the pup tent. As we were setting up, Donna started shouting and leaping up and down. She had accidentally stepped on a hornets' nest and they were buzzing up and down inside her pants. We took her to the local hospital. I don't remember what they did for her, but when we got back to our campsite, she decided to sleep in the car.

3. We went back to this same site several times. One time, there was a huge log by the edge of the river. Donna and I decided we would push the log into the river, straddle it and float away down the river. As we were floating along, the current suddenly picked up. Donna dove off the log and using all her swimming strength, swam to the other side of the river. I

clutched at the sides of the log and as it was speeding along, I saw branches of a tree hanging over the edge and realized the log was going to zip under the branches. I grabbed the branches as far up as I could, and the log whipped out from under me. The water was swirling all around me. I wondered how long I could hang on, how I would get to the shore, and if this was the end of me. After a bit, I looked up and there was Donna, lying down on the bank where the tree was, reaching for me. She was able to pull me onto the shore and then we both started to hug and cry.

4. Another time we were at a different campsite, on a lake. Steve was around 2 or 3 years old. The three of us were sitting on a log in the water with our feet dangling in the water. Well, Steve's feet weren't but Donna's and mine were. Steve was sitting between us and he suddenly slipped into the lake, sinking fast. I literally froze. Donna dived off the log, grabbed him, and carried him sputtering to the surface. He was okay; I wasn't. I never took the children back to that camping spot.

For some reason, Holly never went camping with my grandchildren.

Steve was taken care of by a lovely woman who lived nearby until he started pre-school. He started preschool in September when he was three. He did not say anything or participate in singing until January! The two preschool teachers were wonderful and very kind. Miss Postlewaite and I can't remember the other teacher's name.

I started to do some volunteer work in New Westminster at Woodlands School for the mentally challenged. Eventually, I was hired at Woodlands. I was able to get a grant from the N.D.P. government to help the children on the ward I was on. By the end of

Are you there gin? It's me, Mary Ann at 80.

the grant, these people had grown taller, they were no longer eating with their hands and some of them were toilet trained. I was quite pleased with these accomplishments for the staff and the children.

I also set up a program for another group of children to go to the Federal Prison in Matsqui, once a week, to practice their social skills with "lifers." Training the men was interesting for me and they needed to learn to enunciate as they spoke, so the child assigned to them would understand them.

The men treated me with respect and were wonderful with the children. At first, the guards walked around on an upper level of the gym, but soon the guards realized nothing untoward was going to go on and stopped watching us.

The prisoners could not have any fresh fruit, which I thought was dreadful. So, on one of my trips, I put a pound of Bing cherries in my briefcase and a plastic bag labelled "pits". The guards had stopped searching my case, so I was able to get the cherries into the gym. Very soon, one of the lifers brought me my empty case, saying they had "taken care of the cherries." The prisoners were worried I might "get caught!" I have no idea what they did with the cherries or the pits.

Some of the men who worked with children with mental challenges were able to get passes to leave the federal jail for short times. I would often give them a ride into Vancouver to their halfway house.

A few times we had picnics in Stanley Park. One of the men said, "This is the only time I've been in Stanley Park when I wasn't breaking into cars!"

Other men were able to get out of jail on parole.

How often have you made very bad decisions in your life? Well, I certainly did.

One of the criminals on parole started living with me and my children. He was in jail for armed bank robbery. While we were living together, his parents came to visit him. They were delightful people and it was hard for me to understand why this guy turned out so badly. My refrigerator stopped working while they were visiting, and his father kindly bought me a new refrigerator.

Robber man told me he was looking for a job. He would leave early in the morning and return around dinner time. Somehow, he never got a job. Lord knows what he was doing or where he was doing it during the day. He wanted me to buy him steel toe boots for some job he was applying for. I didn't.

He received a letter at my house, from a pawn shop in a nearby community. I asked him about this. He had pawned my diamond engagement ring! And I still let him live in our house!

I was storing a car for a man from Australia who was working in the North West Territories. I kept the car keys hidden from robber man. At one point he found them and drove the car to another community, far away. I reported this to the police, complete with his name, description, and the description of the car. They found the car and returned it to me but did not arrest him. And I still let him live in our house!

During the time robber man was living with me and my children, robber man and I were asked to stand up for a couple who wanted to get married in the Unitarian Church. The groom was permanently out of jail, had a job, and was able to support his bride.

My children were with their father over the long weekend. I felt totally stressed and depressed about being divorced, living with a criminal; I felt I was not a good mother, and decided to commit suicide. My doctor had prescribed Valium for me. I swallowed the remaining pills in the bottle and lay in my bed waiting to die.

The next thing I knew robber man was yelling at me to get up and get ready for the wedding. I could barely move. I was able to get dressed and he drove my car to the church. I had to have help standing, did not remember what I was supposed to say at

Are you there gin? It's me, Mary Ann at 80.

the wedding and I still don't remember what happened after the wedding.

Now I wonder if the minister was aware of my condition. As the drug wore off, I remember thinking I needed to get my act together. If I couldn't even commit suicide, there must be something I could do as a better alternative. But I still let robber man live in our house!

One evening, while playing bridge with our neighbors, robber man said he would go to my basement and take the clothes out of the dryer. Thoughtful guy. It seemed to me to take an awfully long time for him to do this. I finally went down to see what was going on. There he was with a rubber tube around his arm, shooting heroin into his vein! I couldn't believe it.

I didn't know he was a drug addict besides an armed bank robber, a liar and a cheat. The next day, I packed up his few possessions and dumped them on the lawn of the half-way house, never to see him again.

When I told my children why I had kicked robber man out, my daughter said, "Mom, Wendy, and I found a hypodermic needle and spoon in the basement rafters, but we didn't tell you."

A few days after I kicked him out, there was a loud knocking at my door. I opened it and saw two burly policemen standing there. They asked if robber man lived here. Fortunately, robber man didn't. They told me if he did live with me, they might raid my house and ruin some of my things while looking for his drugs!

I was so glad I had taken his meager possessions to the half-way house. Staying with him could have ruined my professional reputation besides numerous other valuable opportunities that came into in my life.

While I was working at Woodlands, I had the opportunity to go to the North West Territory to assess a young girl with mental challenges.

I flew to Fort Churchill then took a small plane to Chesterfield Inlet, which had one landing strip and no lights. The community is on the western shore, ½ way up the Hudson Bay. There were no cars, no traffic lights but lots of snowmobiles.

Later, I did another assessment in Rankin Inlet and I helped a teacher in Frobisher Bay, which is now called something else.

When I was in Chesterfield Inlet, there were several language people there, hoping to develop a program using the Inuit's native tongue. I told them the girl I was helping called me, "Nut-nut" or something like that. They told me either she called me, "mama" or she called me a "big shit." Talk about the importance of enunciation!

A group of us were going to camp on a little island, visible from the Chesterfield shore on the weekend. We would need a boat to take us and our gear. We bartered with a man who had a motor-boat, giving him steaks. He gave us a ride.

However, a barge came in the night before we left, bringing alcohol.

On our trips to and from the island, the boat was weaving back and forth in the water!

And the mosquitoes were monstrous!

On the island, we saw stone Inukshuks in honor of the deceased.

There were no trees or porta-potties on the island. It was an adaptive and itchy experience!

In Chesterfield Inlet, I saw a man carving a soapstone bird, perched over eggs formed from deer antler. I bought this carving from him for $25! I so wish I had taken a picture of him carving this. It is now on a shelf in our condo and I have no idea what it is worth in today's market.

On one of my trips to Chesterfield Inlet, I was snowed in. I was delayed getting home by two days. In preschool, son Steve drew a picture of several children sitting around a table. He used a black

Are you there gin? It's me, Mary Ann at 80.

crayon to draw the children. And he told Miss Postlewaite, "These are children who don't have any mommies."

My very first Christmas as a single parent, I decided to take my kids skiing at Mount Baker and planned that we'd stay in a motel and find a restaurant serving Christmas dinner. Because we were going to be gone awhile, our refrigerator was fairly empty.

When we got to Mount Baker, I discovered it was closed for the American holidays! And none of the hotels or motels had vacancies for us. So, I drove home and we ate hot dogs for Christmas dinner.

Steve was six years old and I could just hear his first-grade teacher asking the class to tell about their Christmas happenings!

I heard there was a psychology job available at B.C. Children's Hospital and I applied for it. My interview was at the end of the day. I was tired and rather scared. I was interviewed by the president of the hospital and two doctors.

I didn't think I sold myself very well and I called one of the doctors the following day to tell him some of the things I accomplished at Woodlands. Well, he said he wasn't at the interview! Then I was sure I would NOT get the job, but I did get the job, and started working there fulltime in 1974.

While I was working at Children's Hospital, which was a 45-minute drive from our house, Steve's feet broke out in a dreadful rash. Holly called me and said the school called our house to have me pick him up as he couldn't walk.

I had Steve put in a cab and delivered to Children's. This way, I could see him during the day and Holly in the late afternoon and evening.

He was in a room with another little boy. Both of them had to stay in bed, but they entertained themselves by throwing spitballs at each other. One of the cleaning staff ladies chastised me about my son's behavior.

A few staff and I made a film to educate children about being in the hospital. Steve was the star, falling off his bike and pretending to break his leg. He had a cast put on (and later, sawed off). I had a pretend husband (one of the photographers) and we visited Steve in a hospital bed, etc.

A nurse and I went to several hospitals in BC communities to educate staff about helping children in their hospital, using this film.

In the late '70s, there was talk about a new Children's Hospital being designed. I was working on the Teen Unit at this time.

The architect and program manager were coming to interview us about what teens needed when in hospital. I was sitting next to the teen psychiatrist when Ian and a huge woman stormed into the room. I said to the psychiatrist, "Well that's one man I will not mess with." Ian and I were married eighteen months later, final proposal #7. And seven is my very lucky number, in fact 07 was my Psychological Registration Number.

In 1979, I decided to go to UBC and get my doctorate, even though I was a registered psychologist with my masters.

Holly and Steve agreed to live in student housing, so I sold the house, (I remember Foster thinking my first husband gypped him financially) stored a lot of our things and moved to UBC. I took the entire required psychological course work and enjoyed being at university but did not pass one of my exams.

I dropped out of UBC and I then applied for and received a job at Richmond Family Services, where I supervised several psychologists.

The previous year, Holly had a major operation at the University of Washington, to correct the bridge of her nose.

She enjoyed going to high school at U Hill, where she got lots of attention from her male peers. Steve made good friends with Wade, a boy across the way from us, and Steve adjusted well to U Hill Elementary School.

Are you there gin? It's me, Mary Ann at 80.

I think my decision to move to UBC was good for the children and me. This leads to the next chapter!

CHAPTER 9

Early Life with Ian

If you can't laugh at yourself, let me do it.
~ Seen on T-shirt

IAN AND I WERE both on the original Ronald McDonald House Committee for Vancouver. This was another opportunity to get to know one another.

I was president of an association providing help to children in hospitals. Most of the other members were nurses. I asked Ian to join this association. He requested I write him a letter about why he should join the organization.

I saw him the following week and I asked him where his dues were. He asked me where his letter was. He got his letter the next day, and I got his dues.

While president of this organization, I submitted a couple of papers, and they were accepted for presentation at an international convention in Washington D.C. I do not remember what research I did but I remember submitting the briefs before the research was done! Totally pathetic.

The BC Provincial Health Department asked me to present to them what children needed in the hospital. I thought of the three

Are you there gin? It's me, Mary Ann at 80.

people in the organization I knew who were smart and would help me prepare my presentation, one of them being Ian. They were great at helping me prepare. I offered all three a ride to Victoria and Ian was the only one who accepted. Personally, I felt he should have offered me a ride as he had "more money than I did."

My presentation was well accepted. There was a reception in Victoria, after the presentation. Ian schmoozed with numerous people he knew. I helped people with their drinks! After the reception, as Ian and I were waiting for the ferry back to Vancouver, my hand was on the gearshift of my car, and all of a sudden, Ian's hand was on top of mine. Thank heavens I don't have a heart condition!

On Ian's and my first "real date" we went to see the movie *Casablanca*. I think I was more interested in Ian than in the movie.

Not too long after that, the first meal I cooked for Ian was shrimp and a salad. He brought the shrimp and I got the white wine. He told me his favorite white wine was Pouilly-Fuissé, so I bought it. It was DREADFUL with the shrimp, but he was smitten enough not to complain.

At another meal I was fixing for Ian in my tiny university apartment kitchen, the fat in the frying pan caught fire. I grabbed the first potted plant I could find and dumped it on the fire. Ian told me he was impressed with my decision.

The first Christmas we were "well into a serious relationship," I asked him what he was giving me for Christmas. He said he wouldn't tell me, so I asked him if he would answer some simple questions. He said, "Yes." Was the gift from a jewelry store? Yes. Was the gift in a small box and round? Yes. Later, out of Ian's earshot, I called a girlfriend and I said I was getting engaged at Christmas.

So, I opened my Christmas gift from Ian and there was a lovely WATCH.

The Shellers announced they were coming to Vancouver to meet this person I kept writing to them about.

I mentioned to him that he better put food in his apartment refrigerator as my mother would want to see his apartment and would look in his refrigerator.

We were living together by then. And I said we better set a wedding date, even though I didn't want to get married, Ian did. Both of us for the same reasons; which I don't even want to go into now.

We threw a dart at the calendar and it landed on March 17, which was not the best date for us as Ian's first wife is from Ireland. So, we chose March 18th. Ian put his shaving stuff in my medicine cabinet and his shirts in my closet. And true to form, my mother asked to see Ian's apartment and pulled open the refrigerator door as soon as she entered.

Ian took my father out for lunch and mentioned we were getting married. My father said, "Well, she's not easy to live with." I had not lived at home since I was 17, and here I was, 40 years old! My mother was thrilled we were getting married.

When I was driving my parents back to the airport, my mother said, "Dear, I know it's none of my business, but I wonder if you and Ian are living together." She figured this out because Ian picked them up from their hotel in the morning and brought them to me in student housing, then drove to work. If he had been living in his apartment, it would have been one heck of a lot of driving for him.

When Ian and I got married, my parents were thrilled! My sister and all three of my nieces came to the wedding. My niece, Lynne, came to Vancouver with her first baby, Rachel.

The night before our wedding, Ian told me he quit his job. I said, "Don't tell my father." I was worried sick how we would "make it" and had visions of us living in a tent on my salary. However, Ian set up a private practice, and obviously, things worked out.

Are you there gin? It's me, Mary Ann at 80.

At our wedding luncheon, my father called Ian "Ivan." Ian referred to him as "Mr. Shelley," and my mother continued to call Ian I-an. Holly sang at our wedding and Rob L, a psychology graduate student in my class, married us. A wonderful event for both Ian and me.

We had our wedding reception at the UBC graduate center on a Wednesday night, because we thought people would go home early. Everyone we invited came! It was great fun. Steve and his friends threw bread rolls at each other (Ian and I didn't see this but heard about it later). My father finally asked Ian and me to leave as he wanted to go to bed!

As we were leaving, Emma clung to Ian. I told Emma twice, that Donna, my maid of honor, would take her home. She didn't let go of Ian's arm. I was sure this was going to be a problem. But the kids had decorated our car and Emma wanted to see Ian's face when he saw the car! She ran back to the rest of the group laughing.

Donna wore the only dress she's ever worn! While taking our children home, she literally drove Holly, Steve and Emma across campus and had a flat tire. This meant she had to take all the wedding presents out of the trunk, get the spare tire and change it. I think our children heard every swear word Donna ever knew.

Our wedding rings are engraved with MAGIC. This means marriage, accountability, goodness, integrity, commitment or MAGIC or Mary Ann George Ian Carter.

Ian and I went to Harrison Hot Springs for our honeymoon.

We made a reservation to have dinner in the fancy dining room and dance. Before this, we each had a massage. Ian said he was quite uncomfortable after his massage and could barely dance. The following morning, we called two physiotherapists we knew in Vancouver for some suggestions for Ian's pain. Their suggestions didn't work, so we cut our honeymoon time short, asked the two physios to meet us at our house about the time we would get there.

I had to drive, and every bump hurt Ian. My family was kind and did not make jokes about Ian being in pain after the first night of our honeymoon, at least in front of us. It only took one of the physio's to successfully treat Ian.

Our early years together were filled with our passion for each other, our determination to make our second marriage work, adjusting to our different ways of doing things, Ian getting used to fathering my children, keeping his relationship with his daughter strong, and learning to appreciate each other's strong points and ignoring that which we can't change in the other.

CHAPTER 10

Adjusting to My New Marriage in the '80s

*Some days the supply of curse words
is insufficient to meet my demands.*
~ Seen on T-shirt

IAN AND I (WELL Ian) rented a large house on Acadia Road on campus. I got my things out of storage and it was fun having nice things again. We had some great parties at this house.

One Christmas, I bid on the French horn section of the Vancouver Symphony and won. They came to our house, along with their spouses. We had a delightful dinner, probably more than enough booze, along with the Vancouver Symphony drummer and his wife. We played Christmas carols and we recorded some of us singing along. Thankfully, not me.

One night, Holly made macaroni and cheese for us for dinner. Ian was furious. He hates macaroni and cheese. He stormed out of the house, spewing gravel in the driveway and didn't come home until quite late. The problem was I love macaroni and cheese, as does Holly and neither of us knew Ian didn't. We wondered where

Are you there gin? It's me, Mary Ann at 80.

he had gone and why he was so angry, but we enjoyed our dinner. Steve must have been out for dinner.

So, in a very mature way, after Holly and Steve went to bed, I took refuge on the living room couch with a blanket, hoping Ian might be a tad concerned about "where I was" when he returned. I can't remember what happened, but it reminded me of a joke in the New Yorker, showing a father and son looking at two framed pistols. The mother is in a chair with a patch over her eye and the father has a claw for a hand. The father is saying, "These are the very weapons your mother and I used in our famous duel"; which shows you one of the benefits of a long marriage.

When Steve entered high school, Ian and I felt it best for him to have our same last name to save him problems describing why his name was different than ours.

Ian met with Steve's birth father to discuss this and he agreed. We asked the minister who married us to come and baptize Steve with his new name. Steve wanted his birth father to be there and Steve's friend Wade, besides Holly and us. Rob L., the minister, and his wife gave Ian and me a crockery bowl for our wedding present. We used this bowl for the baptism water, in our backyard on Acadia. Steve and Nancy now have this bowl.

The first day Steve went to high school, he forgot to take his bike lock and his bike was stolen. Ian was totally generous, as usual, and bought him a brand-new bike. I couldn't believe it. Talk about love and understanding. Ian placed Steve's new bike in the trunk of his car and told Steve to get something for him from this trunk. We watched from the window as Steve opened the trunk. He looked at Ian and Steve couldn't believe it.

Holly was accepted into the University of Victoria. She lived with a divorced woman during her first year but was able to get into student housing after that, where she met her good friend, Sharon.

When Holly decided to get a second degree from U of Vic, she was not healthy and was diagnosed with Crohn's Disease. While waiting for her operation, she took care of the aged in the hospital (a hospital Ian previously made renovations to) while the medical staff were waiting for her health to be safe enough to operate. When she had her operation, she had part of her colon removed. This chronic problem still flares up when she is under pressure, but she **never** complains about it.

Ian and I went to her second graduation and saw Magna Cum Laude after her name. We were totally impressed. She returned to Vancouver and got an apartment with Sharon.

The jobs she was able to find were barely providing her with enough money to get by, while paying for her student loans. At one point she asked me for financial help, but I, too, was unable to financially help her.

She had one job as manager of the new Ronald MacDonald House, then as a clown for others' festivities, etc.

Ian wanted a new car, so he gave Holly his "old" car. Grateful as she was for the gift, Holly was so poor, she couldn't afford to drive the car, so left it in the alley behind their apartment, where it was eventually towed away.

Holly got a teaching job in Burnaby and never looked back. She received a third degree from UBC as a librarian.

Early in our marriage, four female friends and I decided to take a trip to Santorini, Greece, and three of us would go on to Turkey. The trip was great fun for all of us. Ian was a gem and helped me financially to go on this trip.

We took the ferry from Santorini, Greece to Ephesus, Turkey, and loved looking at the ruins. We went to a carpet place and I bought a runner for our hall that fit perfectly when I returned to our house. The carpet is now on our condo kitchen floor. As we were getting

Are you there gin? It's me, Mary Ann at 80.

on the bus to Izmir, one of the carpet men ran alongside the bus, shouting at one of us, "Marry me, marry me."

There was a male parade happening in Izmir we didn't quite understand. Fancy convertibles would come into the square, the men and boys would get out and dance, then proceed ahead. Three policemen were watching and following us. We finally asked them what was going on. Apparently young teenage boys are circumcised, and this is a celebration of them coming into manhood! OUCH. We gave the policemen our business cards and months later, they sent us an envelope with three postcards in it wishing each of us happy birthday.

The three of us went to dinner at a snazzy restaurant in Izmir at 5 p.m. We were the only ones there and had trouble reading the menu. We ordered what we thought looked like a chicken dish. The food was fine. When we tried to pay the bill, for some reason my credit card wouldn't work, and we didn't have any Turkish money. They finally just said for us to go! We couldn't believe it. Would this happen in your town?

I contacted Belin Goren, a friend from Istanbul who had lived in the states with her family. Belin and I met in high school. In 1955, she came from Turkey to Wauwatosa as a foreign exchange student. The family she was staying with was away, so she stayed with me (and my dreadful parents). Belin said she would pick us up at the Istanbul airport.

We were late getting to the reception area at Istanbul Airport as our plane baggage door was stuck. Once we were in the area, there was no one who looked like her, so we got a cab and gave the driver the address of our hotel.

It was a teeny hotel next to a bar. We asked the cab driver to wait while we checked out of our room. The clerk behind the desk confirmed our reservation. Then we tried to figure out how much we owed the cab driver. The clerk went to the bar next door and found someone who spoke a little English to help us. The cab driver took money out of his pocket to show us how much we owed him. One of us took this money, thinking it was our money. We hadn't paid him yet. We didn't get into an altercation, but it was very close.

We asked the clerk if the hotel restaurant was open, but no, it was midnight and the restaurant was closed and there was no restaurant open nearby. We went to our room and drank everything in the little refrigerator. Soon there was a knock at our door and the clerk was there with three pieces of cake he found in the restaurant kitchen. How kind is this!

The next day we did touristy things and a young man started hanging around with us. We finally connected with Belin. She made a reservation for us at a restaurant for dinner. This meant we needed to take two cabs to the ferry to get to the restaurant. In the middle of heavy traffic, Belin leaped out of one cab to tell the other driver we were going to a different ferry as the first one was too crowded. Then the piles of food she ordered for us started appearing and it was overwhelming. She was totally over generous.

When we returned to Greece to meet our other two friends, our clothes were getting a tad ratty. I had a black cotton dress that was more bag-like and by the end of the trip, each one of us had worn it! Needless to say, the dress went into the garbage before we returned to Vancouver.

In 1983, Ian and I decided to become Canadian citizens so we could vote federally and confirm our commitment to each other. Steve and Holly both joined us in this ceremony. When the judge was talking to all of us who were becoming Canadians, he described a family with an architect, a psychologist, a U of Vic college student and another child who looked like he would become a university student. I leaned over and said to Holly, "There is another family here who are just like us." She said, "Mother, he's talking about us!"

Are you there gin? It's me, Mary Ann at 80.

The judge and R.C.M.P. officer came to shake our hands, welcoming us as citizens. He first greeted Steven Ace Carter, then George Ian Carter, then Mary Ann Sheller Carter, then Holly Sheller Ace. He was a bit confused by all of our names but said, "I'm sure you have it all figured out."

In 1984, Ian was hired as Director of Planning and Design and architect in charge of planning and designing guidelines for buildings from participating countries and site layout for Vancouver Expo '86. This was a wonderful time for us as we met many people from many countries and my student wardrobe got replaced with "adult" clothing.

When Expo opened, the Shellers came to visit us and my father loved everything about it. I think the fact he was connected to Ian and got into the displays without waiting in line, helped that happen.

Holly's friend, Sharon, lived with us for a while, while she was working at UBC. She told me she didn't want to marry her sweetheart until he could give her a substantial engagement ring. I told her the story of my Christmas watch and said I didn't have an engagement ring.

Ian must have overheard our conversation as a few weeks later, he asked me to marry him. I told him we were already married, then I realized, there was more to this conversation than I thought at first.

I lovingly accepted his proposal and he lovingly gave me an engagement ring. So, we started our relationship with children, then got married, then engaged!

CHAPTER 11

The Carter's Life in the '90s

*A little gray hair is a small price
to pay for all this wisdom!
~ Seen on T-shirt*

PROFESSIONALLY, I WAS IN private practice full time. I received clients from many sources. In the mid '80s there was not much research regarding treatment for sexual abuse. A huge sexual abuse case broke in a small community and I became part of a provincial team of professionals to work with the families whose children had been abused by the principal of the local elementary school. This was quite a learning experience. From then on, I received all kinds of sexual abuse referrals for assessments, and I was doing lots of court work. I saw adults and children who were abused and assessed alleged offenders. It was very stressful. A friend suggested I go back and finish my doctorate.

So, at age 50, I took a course in statistics and came out top of the class, after being tutored! I thought my placing might have been a misprint!

Are you there gin? It's me, Mary Ann at 80.

I enrolled in the counselling program at UBC and loved it. There were only three of us in the doctoral program and we were very different from one another. Because I was registered as a qualified psychologist, I didn't have to do an internship, so it only took me four years to complete my doctoral course work and orals, graduating in June 1994.

My advisor, who I had contact with many times before I was in the program, asked me to do some work with the Bella Bella First Nations Heiltsuk community in B.C. What an opportunity he presented to me.

I remember my mother said to me to not walk by an open door. If it doesn't work out, you can always leave, but you may miss out on an opportunity if you walk by.

In November 1999, I was awarded the Park Davidson Award for Significant Contribution to Psychology in British Columbia from the BC Psychology Association and the plaque I was given has this quote on it.

When I flew into the Bella Bella community, I was wearing heels and a dress for my interview with the First Nations Council. I walked into their boardroom. There they were, all sitting around in t-shirts and jeans! I can't believe I was hired to come in for three days each month.

The first client I had in this community came in and talked her head off. After ½ hour she said, "Oh, I feel so much better," got up and walked out. I wondered if she had been paid to do this or was on drugs. Over time, the community accepted me, and I learned so much about the Heiltsuk culture. I feel this opportunity was a win/win situation.

On one of my trips to Bella Bella, I sprained my ankle and could barely walk. One of the women saw me fall, got her car and a frozen salmon and drove me to the plane. She said to put the salmon on my ankle during the flight and cook it when I got home! After having my foot in a cast, I was diagnosed with osteoporosis.

I also had my eyelids lifted by a surgeon in North Vancouver, as I was afraid the children I was treating would think I was close to death and we would not "connect".

There was still some bruising evident on my face from the operation, even with make-up. When I got off the plane, the woman who picked me up was sure my husband had beaten me.

I learned if there is a potlatch happening, don't expect your clients to turn up. Go to the potlatch and gratefully accept whatever is being given out, as the family has been saving for and planning this for years. And eat everything, including seal fat, etc.

We thoroughly enjoyed using our Whistler cabin for a ten-year period. We sold it in 1994 and moved into our home on 27th, the same year Holly got married, I graduated with my doctorate, and Ian's father died. These three events all happened in the same month.

Are you there gin? It's me, Mary Ann at 80.

Holly married Tom Lloyd in an outdoor wedding at Simon Fraser University. Tom was able to help Holly manage her finances, so she is now debt free. Both Holly and Tom had jobs where they could take three years at less pay and have a sabbatical during the fourth year. They did this for a full year, taking Rhys and Julia to numerous European countries, including Egypt.

Steve went to Langara College for two years then transferred to UBC where he majored in sociology, living at home. He had several jobs while he was in college.

At one point he was working at a nearby gas station and was held up. We couldn't understand why it was taking him so long to come home. It was because he was being questioned by the police!

Another job he had was working as a waiter at a White Spot restaurant. He didn't want to take the management training program they offered as he said he made more money waiting tables.

After graduating from UBC, we gave Steve a round-trip ticket to England, his sister gave him a backpack and his birth father gave him a one-month European train ticket. He met his friend, Andrew, in Europe, and the two of them were able to travel around for several months, having a variety of experiences. Steve was robbed as he slept on one of the trains, but his passport was not stolen.

He was interested in computers and took a training course which led to him being hired by a company helping to set up the Vancouver airport computer system. While he was working there, he was asked to be a consultant to an airport in Washington, D.C. Eventually, the firm Steve was working for was no longer needed at the Vancouver airport, so he was let go. He had worked for them long enough; he had good severance pay.

Steve met Nancy at a stoplight, while he was cruising downtown Vancouver with a friend. After being together for a while, they decided to get married in Maui. The Vancouver photographer they were going to use, was going to be in Maui at the same time! Their best wedding photograph has a man in the distant background, in the sea, looking down with his hands in front of him…Lord knows why this wasn't erased!

At any rate, this photographer captured Ian's and my wedding, Holly and Tom's wedding, and Emma and Vinicio's wedding, so we refer to him as our family photographer.

The job Steve has now, he thoroughly enjoys. He is working with personnel and computers for a firm that handles land titles. In fact, in 2015, he was awarded the Collaboration Award. In 2019, he was awarded the Leadership Award. These awards were voted on by his peers.

Emma graduated from Simon Fraser University with a degree in English and a Certificate in Liberal Arts. She applied for a job at Safeway but scored too high on the tests to be employed! She agreed to sell long distance phone plans on a door-to-door basis. During this job, she met a B.C. Telus man who gave her his business card and told her to apply for a job. After a week of testing, Emma received her job and worked there for 21 years.

During this time, she participated in salsa dancing lessons where she met her former husband, Vinicio. They married in 1996 and divorced in 2002.

Emma was eventually let go from Telus, but, like Steve's situation, she had great severance pay and was able to find another job at B.C. Hydro.

CHAPTER 12

Mary Ann's Running and the Pink Sweater

Does running late count as exercise?
~ Seen on T-shirt

I WENT TO VISIT the Shellers several times at their home, and later at their nursing home. On one of these occasions, Mother gave me a horrible knit pink sweater I would never be caught dead wearing. Before I flew back to Vancouver, I put the sweater in a bag and dropped it off at Claire's home as a thank you gift for the luncheon she treated me to. Remember this.

At the same time in Vancouver, 1996, a friend and I were doing aerobics at a nearby gym. We were always the last ones back to the gym when we were running. So, we decided to stop going to the gym and just go to one another's homes to run in the morning.

Then, in 1997, I discovered the Vancouver Sun newspaper had a training program at many community clinics for the Sun Run. I signed up for the training at a community centres close to us.

Are you there gin? It's me, Mary Ann at 80.

The training was wonderful, but unfortunately, I was unable to run in the Sun Run as I had to look after Mother in Arizona when Father had a hernia operation.

The next 10k run I participated in was in a community close to where we lived. When the winners were announced, I came in 2nd place for women aged 55-60. This was because there were only two women in this age category! My time was 58:58.

The woman who came in 1st place was 5 minutes faster and 5 years older than me. This time and age difference encouraged me to run faster. I started entering various training programs and entering all kinds of distance races, running faster and faster. There were 5k, 8k, 10k races all around the city. My fastest 10K time was 50 minutes.

In one of the training programs I was in, I found out about British Columbia Senior Track Competition. I entered twice and won several gold medals in the Provincial competitions. And I met many fine running friends, older and younger.

Review Footwerks Labour Day 8K

Colin Dignum punched a hole in the field staying ahead of Bertrand Plouvier's 25:08 runner-up spot. Dignum - who sometimes substitutes as a hill climber - mounted a 25:06 offensive for the win. Coming off the island for a runner's holiday put Neil Holm in third place at 25:18. Ken Bell continues to look impressive as a masters runner clocking 26:04 in this effort. Dave Reed just entering the 45-49ers took first place in 26:50.

Nancy Tinari (40-44) continues to add the notches to her gunslinger's belt with another trouncing of the men and women around her. Her time for the 8k was 27:21. Trailing this dominating runner in were Cari Rampersad (28:30), and chasing her to the line was Erin Heffring in 28:39.

Ian Fisher (28:38) and Herb Philips (28:55) continue to carry the masters lead for the 50s & up with Fraser Valley runner Paul Watkin not far off their pace with his own 29:52. Bonni Walker cut the distance down and took her age group (45-49) in 31:11. Over 50 and Jane Wintemute was looking good with her 38:11 group win. In the women's 55-59 group Mary Ann Carter took a 42:29 first place shot at things.

I also took marathon training. I figured if I could run 10K, running 26.2 miles was possible.

1998 – First 1/2 Half Marathon
TIME: 2:03:00   PACE: 09:22
OVERALL: 1130/1455   CAT: 2/9
SEX: 450/688

Vancouver was my first ½ Marathon in 1998. My time was 2:03:00 and I came in 2nd out of 9 women in my age category.

My first full marathon was the Vancouver Marathon. Gratefully, Holly, Rhys, and Ian were at the finish line to greet me. I was dehydrated and cramped up dreadfully. I was taken to the medical tent where electrolytes were put back into my system. After two bags, I felt I could run the whole thing again! But, certainly never again did I become dehydrated in running my next 10 marathons.

I decided one of my goals would be to qualify for the Boston Marathon. To do this, I had to run a full marathon in 4 hours and 12 minutes. I walked the Portland Marathon due to a pelvic stress injury, and I trained for the marathon by running in the water, wearing a water belt.

There was a wonderful motivational speaker at the 2nd Maui Marathon I ran. I asked him if he would coach me to qualify for Boston. He did and in my 2nd Portland Marathon, I qualified, October 1, 2000.

The finishing times are regularly posted at marathons. When I saw my name, and no one else's, it took me a few minutes to realize I won in my age group and qualified for Boston. I finished in my

Are you there gin? It's me, Mary Ann at 80.

age group in 1st place in 4 hours and 7 minutes. I was thrilled and in tears.

One of the women I ran with in Vancouver wanted to go to Boston with me so she asked me to wait a year so she could qualify for Boston, too.

In 2002, we prepared to go to Boston.

About two weeks before the race, a package arrived from Boston, addressed to me. The return address was the Boston Marathon address. I tore into the package, very excited, and there was a letter with the Boston Marathon logo addressed to me, saying I was one of a few who were lucky enough to receive this gift from the Marathon organizers.

It was the awful pink sweater I spoke of earlier. Claire sent it to her son, who lives in Boston, asking him to do the dirty work and send it to me. I laughed until I was crying. Ian took a picture of me wearing the sweater at the end of my Boston Marathon run. Unfortunately, we can't find the picture.

I came in 13th in my age bracket out of 29 women, which is a tad shabby, but I did it!

A few years later, a young relative of Claire's from Florida, came to a workshop in Vancouver. We got together a couple of times while she was here.

She visited Claire, shortly before she came to Vancouver. I gave her the dreadful, pink sweater and asked her to send it to Claire from Florida as a thank you gift for staying with Claire. She did.

I don't remember how Claire got the pink sweater back to me, but the next time I sent it to her, I looked up when the Wauwatosa City Council met and copied their logo onto a formal letter.

On the internet, I found the Mayor's name and wrote a formal letter to Claire, saying she was voted Senior Citizen of the Year by the Wauwatosa Council, etc. I sent this to Jean, her daughter in

Wauwatosa, and asked Jean to drop it off on Claire's doorstep. She did.

Claire has this awful pink sweater now.

My running career was wonderful. I did 2 marathons in Vancouver, 2 marathons in Victoria, 2 marathons in Maui, 2 in Portland, 1 in Sarasota, Florida and of course the Boston Marathon. I did 1 marathon in Laussane, Switzerland.

The charity we were supporting was diabetes. Each participant needed to raise $5,000. I was able to get donations from friends for up to $2,000. I decided I would give one week's salary to my donation pile. I let each client know about this and gave them a receipt. One of my wealthier clients asked me how much more money I needed. I told him around $3,000. He immediately wrote a cheque for $3,000! I'm surprised I didn't faint.

Lausanne, Switzerland was fun for all of us. Our hotel, *A La Gar*, was right next to the train station, so sleeping was a challenge. During the race, we ran through small towns with people sitting at little tables drinking coffee, tea, and wine, cheering us on. We ran on a wide path next to Lake Geneva on one side and a high hill on the other. Then we all turned around and ran back. Very lovely. As we were running along, several yodelers in the hills sang to us.

Are you there gin? It's me, Mary Ann at 80.

During my running years, my son, Steve, gave me a gift certificate to climb Grouse Mountain. The two of us did this. I wanted to do it in less than an hour. I started out running. After five steps, I stopped running and started climbing! We made it in just over an hour. At one point, I wondered if Steve was hoping for his mother to have an early demise.

Ian and I decided to train for triathlons. This meant swimming, running and biking. For one of my birthdays, Ian arranged for me to have a snazzy bike made to fit me. I thoroughly enjoyed biking. I kept up my running and took swimming lessons. We entered a bike/run in Penticton, some short tri's at UBC, and I entered a tri in Penticton.

During the Penticton swim, for some reason, I was unable to move forward. I thought of the hill I was going to have to bike up, panicked and got out of the water, quitting the race. I continued to train for tri's in Vancouver, swimming in the ocean.

On one swim, going from buoy to buoy, I thought one of the other swimmers was behind me. When I got to the buoy, I saw it was not a swimmer; it was the resident seal. Once again, I panicked. Did the seal have bad eyesight and seeing me in a black wet suit thought perhaps he/she had a playmate?

The tide was coming in, so I was sure I could float back into shore if necessary. I noticed the lifeguard hauling a rowboat to the shore. He was coming to rescue me. No way. As he neared me, I mentioned the seal and said I would float in, slowly. The seal had disappeared.

When I got to shore, a couple was watching me come in. She came up to me and said her husband was getting ready to swim out to help me just before the lifeguard appeared. What kind folks they were.

I successfully completed the Vancouver triathlon, slowly, but successfully. In fact, Ian needed to ask the staff to please leave the timer up as I was still on the course.

I think of my elementary school years when I was always the last in the class to be chosen for any athletic team. Then in my late '50s training to run fast and enjoying it.

At the start of my running life, I would usually come in second or third in my age category. I decided to think "come in first." And this seemed to work for me, as I did start coming in first.

On August 10, 2002, I competed in the 5K Sausage Race in Milwaukee, WI. I was in Wauwatosa for a high school reunion. Several of us walked or ran the race. I came in 1st out of 10 in my age group, 26:12 minutes.

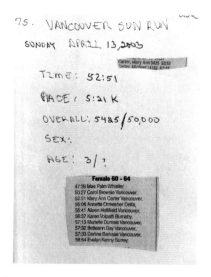

Now being in the 60-64-year age group, the "real" runners competed! I ran the Sun Run in April 2003 finishing at 52:51, coming in third in my age group. There were 50,000 runners. During the run, I felt like most of them passed me.

The last run I kept a record of was a 10K I ran in November 2004, when I was 64. I came in 2nd out of 10 other old women!

As my arthritis began to creep up on me, I decided to stop running and doing tris. I enjoyed these activities for ten years.

P.E.O. is something I thoroughly continued to enjoy as my running life drew to a close.

CHAPTER 13

P.E.O.

*Twinkle, twinkle little star, point me
to the nearest bar.
~ Seen on T-shirt*

MY GRANDMOTHER, MOTHER, SISTER, and three nieces were all P.E.O.s but no one would tell me what it really meant. I didn't want to join a secret organization.

I changed my mind in 1985 and I decided to join P.E.O. if there was a chapter in Vancouver. My mother contacted someone in Vancouver who contacted me. I felt I was in a position to donate some of my time and energy to a worthwhile cause my grandmother, mother, sister, and nieces were involved in.

There were almost forty chapters in BC! Being a P.E.O. is wonderful: providing educational opportunities for other women and personal growth for yourself.

I was invited to meet women in three different chapters and finally I decided I wanted to be in Chapter AE.

I was told I had to wait a year to join Chapter AE, as another Vancouver chapter was being formed of women who were relatives to other P.E.O.'s. I knew if I joined this new chapter, I would

Are you there gin? It's me, Mary Ann at 80.

be very active in it and I didn't feel I had the amount of time that might be necessary. I had waited all these years to join P.E.O., waiting one more year didn't matter to me.

In 1986, I was initiated into Chapter AE. The president whispered the real meaning of P.E.O. into my deaf ear. I still didn't know what P.E.O. meant. I was too unfamiliar with my sisters to ask anyone. I found out the meaning in 1987 when our chapter initiated another woman.

In 2005, the P.E.O. Provincial Nominating Committee asked me to run for the board. Ian agreed he would support me, which he did, and I was on the provincial board for seven years. I met women from many states and provinces, the information I gained, the deep emotional feelings I experienced for a variety of reasons was / is overwhelming for me. And as a P.E.O., these friendships, experiences, and deep feelings continue in me.

P.E.O. is a totally valuable life-long experience. Joy F, a cousin of Ian's, joined Chapter AX, as did my daughter-in-law, Nancy. Daughter, Holly, joined Chapter Z.

I was totally surprised and pleased when Nancy told us she joined P.E.O. Later, Nancy needed to drop out of her chapter because their meeting time conflicted with her job. I hope she will either rejoin her chapter or a chapter that meets at a better time for her.

In 2004-2005 I was very busy with P.E.O. as the International Convention was going to be in Vancouver. I was a hostess in the hospitality room along with another P.E.O. in my chapter.

Our chapter uses our homes as bed and breakfasts to fundraise. The weekend before the convention began, we had a delightful couple stay with us. Dave was bragging how his wife, Judy, played the piano very well. I knew our Music Director, Heather, needed a pianist. I asked him if Judy would play at this convention.

She said she needed to hear the music. She went over to Heather's. Heather was at work, but her husband said Judy sounded just fine.

They needed to change their air reservations, which travel agent, Wendy, in Chapter AE, took care of.

Dave and Judy stayed in our house (as Ian and I were staying downtown), brought us our mail, drove my car, and became good friends. This is typical of how P.E.O.'s and their loved ones operate.

Ian took a group of men accompanying P.E.O.'s on a tour of the Cannery. On his return, Ian came walking towards me in the hospitality room with an old man. Ian said, 'Look who's here." I looked at the man's name tag and it said, "James B."

Jimmy B. and I went to grade school, junior high, and senior high school together! I must have looked "old" to him, too.

His lovely mother was a P.E.O. and now his wife is a P.E.O. on the east coast. It was quite a surprise to connect with him.

And since then, I've seen him at another International Convention. I can't believe we both grew up in Wauwatosa; Jimmy wound up on the east coast and I wound up on the west coast and we connected at a P.E.O. gathering because he sat next to my husband on the bus.

Are you there gin? It's me, Mary Ann at 80.

The Canadian P.E.O. (Vancouver Chapter A) turned 100 in 2012. Building up to this celebration was exciting. It started out a few of us were going to play some old sing-along songs.

We practiced once a week and played in several nursing homes.

A gentleman told me the first time we performed, "The songs are fine, but you need to play a little faster." We called ourselves, "The Trebles in P.E.O." I jazzed up my Volkswagen Beetle with a treble sign and attached eyelashes above the headlights.

Then we decided to add a bit of history, humor, and costumes to our performance. We had 2 flutes, 1 violin, 1 piano, 1 clarinet, 1 oboe, and a horn. We successfully performed our show with accompanying history slides in Kamloops, Chilliwack, Vancouver, and Victoria. In turn, P.E.O.s brought friends to these performances and some of these women joined P.E.O.

The President of the International P.E.O. Chapter attended Chapter A's 100th birthday party celebration. The dress I wore belonged to a P.E.O. in Chapter AE, who had gone to Chapter Eternal.

I was president of the provincial chapter and Chapter A's board buddy. They asked me to entertain the national president. She came to dinner at our home with a few other P.E.O. s. We had cocktails outside, then a nice dinner inside. The following evening, Ian and

I were having a drink outside and a rat ran across our backyard. I would have DIED if this had happened the night before.

The P.E.O. International Convention was in Saint Louis, Missouri in 2011. Several B.C. P.E.O.'s did a wonderful skit about how Chapter A was formed. The B.C. contingency threw a party for all the Canadian chapter sisters in attendance.

Leading the B.C. delegation into the convention was quite thrilling for me. On the opening night, the provincial/state presidents and organizers march in carrying their province or state flags.

Nancy and I had matching suits we found at a Sears Store in Seattle. They fit us perfectly and were very inexpensive. We still have them but haven't worn them to other P.E.O. conventions as we've had other jobs to do at the conventions.

Following the 2019 Provincial P.E.O. Convention, the new P.E.O. President asked me if I would consider starting a Chapter of P.E.O. on the University of British Columbia (UBC) campus. Well, even before I moved onto the UBC campus, I considered this.

This made a lot of sense to me since Ian and I now lived on the UBC campus in a condo.

Several women in my condo are supportive of P.E.O. and a few want to be part of the new chapter. We need to have around eighteen women who are interested in forming a chapter to begin the chapter.

At the time of this writing, there are thirteen women who are interested in joining this UBC Chapter. We are of varying ages and talents, which is interesting. We will hold our meetings in this building's condos.

During the summer of 2019, we advertised P.E.O. at the UBC Farmer Market. We sold handmade beeswax food wrappers and were able to establish a healthy bank account from our sales. Two women we met at the market want to join the UBC Chapter. One of these women is an herbal specialist. She made four Chapter BQ P.E.O. teas for us to sell at the market. Four P.E.O.'s from other chapters want to transfer to the new chapter due to the time and place we meet.

The UBC Farm Market will become one of our "moneymaking" projects to support the International P.E.O. projects.

At the market, you can sign up to play music. Another violinist and I are considering doing this. We enjoy playing duets.

Several P.E.O. chapters provide financial and emotional support for UBC women students. There are also several P.E.O.s who are on the UBC faculty. It seems most appropriate to have a P.E.O. chapter on campus for residents, faculty, and students to join and, or, receive P.E.O. funding.

If women students join P.E.O. while on campus, when they graduate and move to another province or state, P.E.O. is a wonderful way for them to connect within their new community.

CHAPTER 14

My Musical Life

You are about to EXCEED the limits of my medication.
~ Seen on T-shirt

I MAKE MUSIC! I make music with others, and others make music for me. I began my love affair with music by singing in the Congregational Church Children's Choir. I still have the hymnal with my maiden name, Mary Ann Sheller, printed in gold on the cover.

In 4th grade, some friends loaned my family their Steinway grand. The huge piano looked elegant in our living room. I began piano lessons with Miss H. As my playing grew better, I practiced more and more. I dreamed of becoming a concert pianist. In 6th grade, Miss H. encouraged me to be "evaluated." I had to learn one required song and perform one I wanted to play. The first song had a repeat section that was difficult to "get out of." At the evaluation I was nervous, and I kept repeating and repeating that section. I felt anxious and embarrassed, so I just made up a little piece to end the song. The raters mentioned I had creative talent! I hope you are laughing.

In junior high, 7th grade, I took violin, piano, and drum lessons. The drum lessons didn't last more than a year as my parents couldn't stand listening to me practicing the snare and I hated practicing on the rubber pad. I played an ancient violin. A relative had fiddled on this violin while snaking across the prairies in a Conestoga wagon. I stopped taking violin lessons in high school, but I kept the violin. Over the years I would haul it out and try to remember how to tune it, how to bow and play the notes.

I began taking lessons on this old violin again in the 1980s. The violin was stolen from the back seat of my car in 1982. This loss was painful for me and I felt very guilty for not having locked my car. I never shared this circumstance with my older sister or parents. Ian kindly bought me a violin to play in San Miguel and a violin to play in Vancouver. I treasured both of my violins and the memory of the stolen one. When we permanently left San Miguel de Allende, 2019, I donated my violin to my violin teacher to use as he wished.

I joined an award-winning acapella choir in high school led by Gladys something-or-other. We called her "Happy Bottom" behind her back. We performed three Gilbert and Sullivan operettas, and several concerts: It was disappointing to me to never get the lead part, but I enjoyed singing with the altos.

In the first year in college, I was appointed Class Song Leader. Some of us composed songs and lyrics for our Junior Year Skit and I had fun playing duets with a dorm friend. I loved Music 101, learning about classical musicians and their musical development. My professor suggested I take an independent music course, as a sophomore. The professor supervising me just graduated from the Eastman School of Music in Rochester NY. I chose to study all of Beethoven's Symphonies and decided which one I liked best. I knew his 3rd, 5th and 9th were supposed to be his best. However, listening to the 2nd movement of the 7th Symphony brought tears to my eyes the first time I heard it and my emotional reaction made me focus on the 7th Symphony as being my favorite. At the end of the term, I submitted my typewritten fifty-page paper. When this tome was returned to me, it was marked with an "E." I was aghast. I was so upset I couldn't talk to the professor for a week. I finally crept into her office and stated I didn't think this mark fair for the amount of effort I had put in, the amount of reading/listening I did, and expressing my own opinion, which obviously was different than hers. She changed my mark to a "D." At the time, I thought of the mark as a "Damn her."

It still amazes me to think of Beethoven, old, poor, and totally deaf, composing his 9th Symphony, including a choral section. If my family plans a memorial service for me, I would appreciate the 7th being played.

Through my four years at Wells, I attended numerous classical concerts at Cornell. We heard wonderful musicians, like Yo-Yo Ma and Claudio Arrau. I began to think of music as a universal way to communicate.

During the summer, I attend a wonderful Western Amateur Musicians Camp, for a week at Quest University in Squamish BC. Ian and I tried a week at a musical swing camp, but the jazz level was beyond our ability.

I look forward to taking weekly violin lessons and once a week playing with a senior citizen orchestra and chamber group in Vancouver.

We attend in-home concerts close to our Vancouver condo. Imagine sitting within five feet of these REAL musicians! We can ask questions and talk to them. Totally cool. These concerts are much less expensive and more intimate than attending concerts in major Vancouver theatres.

During the quarantine period in 2020, my music teacher had her violin students, ranging in age from four to eighty years old, record two to three pieces. These performances were shared with one another. We each commented on what we liked about the performance. I realized a seven-year-old and I played the same piece. However, he plays it much faster and better than I do!

Are you there gin? It's me, Mary Ann at 80.

To celebrate my 80th, my marvelous music teacher, her talented twelve-year-old pianist son, my fun violin friend, and I, played an hour concert for family and friends at the home of a couple who lives nearby and hosts professional concerts. I looked forward to surprising our friends and family with our performance. We performed for our friends and family: and they applauded us vigorously. It was great fun, and occurred, unexpectedly, twelve days after my right knee was replaced!

Thinking of this reminds me of another time in my life when Mary Ann and marijuana had a musical experience.

CHAPTER 15

Marijuana, Mary Ann and Music

Patience is a virtue. It's just not one of my virtues.
~ Seen on T-shirt

COUSIN, DALE E. HAD a farm in Dallas Center, Iowa. I remember visiting his farm when I was in junior high school, in the 1950s. Dale drove me around on a tractor. What stood out the most for me was marijuana growing like a weed on the farm. The *Reefer Madness* movie was still popular. I was able to stash a weed in my clothes and sneak into my bedroom. I pulled the cardboard backing out of my suitcase, put the weed in, and replaced the backing.

Back in Wauwatosa, we twelve-year olds got corn cob pipes and tamped the dried weed into them. We lit our pipes and attempted to smoke it. I can still feel the burning at the back of my throat. Did we get high? No.

I had my love affair with marijuana in the mid-70s, as a single parent living in the suburb of Coquitlam, British Columbia. Smoking was out, brownies were in. Having two children who loved brownies, mine were wrapped in foil, theirs were wrapped in Saran Wrap, and both batches rested in the freezer.

Are you there gin? It's me, Mary Ann at 80.

One weekend, I was staying downtown at a convention. I asked a teenage brother of Holly's friend to look after my children. I had only one of MY marijuana brownies left in the freezer.

When I returned the next day, my last brownie was GONE. I was livid. I asked Holly and Steve who ate it. Holly said they gave it to Dave, the sitter, for dessert. I asked them what he did after dinner. They said he sat at the piano and played and played and played, a musical response to getting high. Dave did not babysit another time.

I kept my small stash in a plastic bag in a drawer next to my bed. Holly discovered it when she was in 6th grade. Our neighbor's daughter, Wendy, in 5th grade was in cahoots with Holly. They took some of the marijuana in my bag to the elementary school to sell. Somehow the principal found out about it and called Holly into the office for some serious questioning. Holly put on her most innocent face and pretended not to know anything about what he was saying. I have no idea what happened to Wendy. The principal did not call me. Holly told me about this episode when we were BOTH adults.

My childhood friend, Claire, came to visit me when I lived in Coquitlam. She never smoked marijuana. I got two joints and we went to stay at the fancy Empress Hotel in Victoria. We had a drink and smoked one of the joints. Then our laughter started. We could barely make it across the lobby of the hotel to get a cab to a restaurant to satiate our pot-induced munchies. Unfortunately, Claire didn't particularly like the effects of the joint.

So I thought it would be nice for Claire to take the other joint back to her husband, Ed. She also bought two t-shirts for her twin boys that said, "I had beaver in Vancouver." She went through customs with the joint nestled in with her cigarettes. Remember this was in the '70s.

When she arrived back in Wauwatosa, Ed had a fit. He flushed the joint down the toilet and refused to let her give the t-shirts to their twins. She and I had no idea what was wrong with the t-shirts. We were in our thirties. I thought myself so very worldly...I guess not!

My marijuana stint didn't last long as when I had parties and would use it, I always wound up sleeping on the floor with guests stepping over me saying, "Good night, Mary Ann." I am a party person and enjoy people ...no more special brownies for Mary Ann.

Funny how in 2018, close to 50 years later, marijuana was made legal in Canada.

Aren't any of you wondering where I got my marijuana? I certainly didn't grow it in my backyard. I was working with lifers in federal prison and the men were very generous with their pot. I think the expression is, "if there's a will, there's a way." This led me to another tale about working with these men: which I already described in Chapter 8.

CHAPTER 16

My Health

My body is a TEMPLE: ancient and crumbling.

Seen on T-shirt

WHEN I WAS QUITE young, my mother would take me to Milwaukee Children's Hospital every Saturday morning to have my blood taken by Dr. Z. Dr. Z was ugly. She had thick, dark, curly hair on her chin. After she jabbed me with the needle, she would reach into her pocket and give me a jellybean. I hate jellybeans, except for the black ones. I was anemic. Every day, my mother would give me a spoonful of cod liver oil. I hate cod liver oil.

My tonsils were taken out when I was in elementary school. I was in a ward with other children. This wasn't a playful time.

In the 1960s, as I mentioned earlier, I had a skull fracture, concussion, and all the tendons on my left hand were severed. Friend, Colleen, called my parents as she had to get back to work in NYC. Jack did nothing. Mike sent flowers. My parents came to Nassau and had me medevacked to Miami, none of which I remember. Mother said I was swearing at the Nassau nurses, using words she had never heard. Dang, I wish I could remember this.

Are you there gin? It's me, Mary Ann at 80.

At any rate, when I "came to", my parents were sitting across from me in a darkened hospital room. I said, "Where am I?" Mother started to cry.

After they left, I crawled across the floor to the bathroom, pulled myself up on the sink, looked in the mirror and said to myself, "Not too bad." Then I crawled back to bed and exercised my left-hand fingers. I had trouble remembering words and wondered if I had "lost my four years of college education."

After a few days, we drove to my grandparent's home in Lakeland. My father returned to Wisconsin. My mother wanted me to come back to Wauwatosa, but I knew if I did, I would be forever "captured there." I eventually went back to NYC.

Later on, in the '60s, during my first marriage, I taught kindergarten while my husband studied for his Ph.D. at the University of Minnesota. Being around the young children I was exposed to germs of all kinds. I became very sick with bronchitis and pneumonia. I would just start to get well, return to work and get sick again. My doctor told me if I didn't stay in bed for a month, he would put me in the hospital.

We couldn't afford for me to be in the hospital, so I stayed in bed for a month. Boring as all get out, but I got better.

In my late thirties, I had a hysterectomy due to a series of bad pap smears. Both my parents and sister came to support me and look after Holly and Steve. I taped a note to my belly button the night before my operation that said, "Remember Wreck Beach, 19--." Wreck Beach is a nude beach in Vancouver. After the operation, when the nurse was wheeling me back to my bed, I said, "Did he get the note?" With a smile on his face, the nurse said, "Yes and I think Dr. M. left you a note." After I was back in bed, I whipped up my hospital gown and there was a long fat, wide bandage from my navel to my crotch. Going down the middle of the bandage was a huge ballpoint pen mark with diagonal slashes all the way along. And printing that said, "Oops, sorry I slipped." I burst out laughing, which didn't feel too good. When my doctor and the surgeon came to see me, I asked them if they could take out anything else, as I was enjoying my private room in the hospital and not having to cook, plus the hospital food was quite good. The surgeon laughed and said he could take out my gall bladder, but that never happened.

When my parents came to take me home, I suggested we go downtown to the Spaghetti Factory for dinner. We did this. For some reason my sister left earlier than she had planned to. I think she and our mother had some disagreement but neither of them told me anything about it.

Shortly after Ian and I were married in the '80s, I went to my M.D. as my shoulder hurt. He took one look at me and sent me to a thyroid specialist, having nothing to do with my shoulder. The problem was Hashimoto Syndrome or a tumor on the gland. I was operated on at St. Paul's. Daughter Holly and friend Sharon came to visit and asked what I wanted. They were able to sneak a hot fudge sundae to me. After half my thyroid was removed, I didn't need to take a thyroid supplement.

Towards the end of the '80s, I prepared a delicious salad of chopped Easter eggs, spinach, and leftover salmon. Stepdaughter Emma was with us for the weekend. Shortly after eating, she charged into the bathroom and threw up. All of a sudden, Ian needed to use the other bathroom. I called poison control and was told to get club soda and Gravol pills. Before our conversation ended, I too, raced to the bathroom.

Son, Steve, called and I asked him to bring home Gravol and club soda. When he arrived, he took one look at Ian and called 911. Two ambulances arrived and rushed Ian, Emma, and me to the UBC Emergency Hospital.

Ian and I each had a needle inserted to replace the electrolytes in our systems. There was a drunk in the area who was singing. The nurse told the drunk, "Please be quiet, there is a very sick man in here." Ian needed six or seven bags of fluid. I had two.

Emma and I went home that night, but Ian was not discharged until the following day. Believe me, it was very embarrassing for me to take Emma home and tell her mother what had happened.

In the '90s, I was diagnosed as having osteoarthritis and osteoporosis. I received a variety of treatments, which somewhat helped my bone density. The chips in my right knee were removed but the pain continued.

Sometime in 2017, or 2018, I had cataracts removed from both eyes and a distant and near-sighted lens inserted. When I put on mascara, it is evident which eye has the near-sighted lens! Before the operation, I was extremely nervous. A man went into the room before me and came out very soon after, looking just fine. This relaxed me a tad until I saw the specialist and his assistant. Both were overweight men with huge fingers. It was difficult for me to think of them going into one of my eyes, removing the cataract, and inserting a lens. I had to sit still, not say anything, and zippo…it was done. After the second cataract was done, the specialist told me I had better than 20/20 vision. I'm not sure how this can be, but I don't have to wear glasses anymore. I went to see my ophthalmologist and he used various lenses in his machine, which I realized gave me even better vision. I bought glasses for night driving.

In 2019, I had stem cell replacement, which helped reduce the swelling in my arthritic thumbs. The surgeon refused to inject it into my knees as he said my right knee was bone on bone and the left knee, not much better. He replaced my right knee in September 2019.

Other than the above, I seem to break teeny bones in my right and left feet on a yearly basis by accidentally slamming into furniture!

The Covid-19 coronavirus became a pandemic in the world in March 2020. Fortunately, Ian and I had permanently returned from SMA to Vancouver, prior to knowing about this virus. We quarantined and stayed six feet away from others; the elderly were given special shopping times in the grocery stores. All the schools, universities, concerts, sporting events, gyms, salons, restaurants, theatres (other than the drive-in), camps, day cares, churches and bars were closed. Only essential services remained open, and usually with reduced hours. It amazes me liquor and marijuana stores were viewed as essential services considering liquor was banned in the 1920's and marijuana only recently became legal in Canada. The greatest number of Covid-19 cases occurred in Senior Citizen Homes. Fortunately, BC had a very low rate of the virus.

This was the first pandemic I experienced in my lifetime. Ian and I used Zoom to see/hear family and friends. Ian took two art classes using Zoom. I practiced duets with my friend on Zoom, had my weekly violin lesson on Zoom, worked with my editor on Zoom and had several inexpensive cocktail parties on Zoom

Hopefully, Alzheimer's and senile dementia will never become an additional paragraph in my health chapter.

CHAPTER 17

The Carters in Mexico

My heart says chocolate and wine,
but my jeans say for the love of god woman, eat salad
~ Seen on T-shirt

I'M CHIQUITA BANANA AND *I've come to say....*no, no.

Before 2010, our friends Stephen and Lorne kept encouraging Ian and me to come to San Miguel de Allende, (SMA) Mexico. They had two homes there and felt we would really enjoy the community, the art, and the music. In 2010, we finally decided to go for a week.

We spent most of our week exploring communities around SMA, learning about the history, the culture, the food, and the artwork. We were enchanted and decided to come back the following year. This time we stayed for a month. We found wonderful concerts, art shows and felt comfortable finding our way around town.

Ian began taking art classes. We found a delightful music teacher, Jesus, and took weekly lessons from him with Ian playing the guitar and me playing the violin. Jesus suggested we form a swing band. We loved the idea. David played the sax, Ian the guitar, Laura the drums, Omar the bass guitar, me the violin and Jesus, usually the guitar: three Gringos and three Mexicans, ranging in age from 30-72. We rehearsed once a week at David's.

In SMA there is an open mic theatre on Tuesday nights. For a very few pesos, you get a glass of wine or soda and the opportunity to hear a variety of performances. The first night our swing band performed there, Ian and I arrived first. The manager asked Ian what our name was. Ian said we had no name. The manager introduced us as the Band with No Name.

Later, in a discussion about what we would call ourselves, Laura suggested it sounded better to call ourselves: *La Banda Sin Nombre*. Ian bought black shirts for us to wear with our band name printed on the back. Anyone who came to visit us was forced to attend the theatre and hear us. We played for a few years until Omar disappeared, Laura had a baby and David had a heart attack. I have great memories of how our friendships developed, the fun we had, and the encouragement we received.

On one occasion, Ian, Jesus, and I performed alone at the theatre. I totally goofed one of the pieces Jesus and I played. No one booed.

Our friendships with Jesus, his family and Laura, and her family continued the entire nine years we were in SMA.

We were invited to Laura and Carlo's wedding, the baptism of their baby, and the funeral of Laura's mother. We were invited to Jesus's baby's baptism and Jesus's birthday party.

This inclusion was quite an honor for us. After the wedding and both baptisms there were huge parties, tons of food, lots of laughter, music, and hugs. Their friends wanted to practice their English with us, and we wanted to practice our Spanish with them.

In the third year we were unable to stay in Stephen and Lorne's home as it was rented to others during the time we wanted to be there. Their property manager found another place for us to stay in the middle of town. Besides two bedrooms, it had a casita in the backyard. The cockroaches enjoyed the casita bathtub, so our many visitors stayed in our house.

In Mexico, there are holidays galore and we attended as many of the events as we could to learn more about the Mexican culture. We took Spanish lessons from a variety of people each time we visited. We found the Warren Hardy Spanish classes the most challenging and rewarding. When we returned to Vancouver, we continued to take weekly Spanish classes from Patricia, a local Mexican woman. We met her through Stephen and Lorne.

One summer, Patricia's mother, Esther, was visiting Patricia in Vancouver. She came to our condo for drinks. We had a very good time. She and I enjoyed our gin. I'm sorry I didn't know about

Are you there gin? It's me, Mary Ann at 80.

Empress Gin at that time. This gin was made in the early 1900's to celebrate the opening of the Empress Hotel in Victoria. The gin is blue, and it turns pink when you add tonic to it.

Esther invited us to visit her in Morelia on our return to SMA. We did, and we had a wonderful time.

One of her adult sons let us use his bedroom and bathroom.

Esther has many relatives in Morelia. I think we met all of them. They would come for coffee, take us out for coffee, take us to see various interesting sites around the community, take us to the park where all the bakers were having sales, and to view historical treasures.

Esther drove us back to SMA in her car and stayed with us for a few nights. I was exhausted and wound up staying in bed one day while Esther, with Ian and without Ian, explored the SMA community. She was a bundle of energy. She intended to visit another daughter in a nearby community, but someone called and told her - get this - "Your father is not feeling well." I'm sure Esther was in her seventies which would put her father well into his nineties, living alone, but I think he had a housekeeper to cook, do his laundry, and clean his house.

The only mail we ever received in SMA was a Christmas card from Esther. I have no idea who put it through our mail slot as there are not postmen/women I know of. I wondered if Esther was traveling to see her other daughter and dropped it off. I wouldn't doubt it.

Writing this leads me to share some of what we learned from our Mexican friends and experiences. Mexicans value family, religion, kindness, children/seniors, respect, and laughter. I think of the numerous struggles these people experienced over the ages, but these basic values are still there. It must be part of their DNA.

When we first came to SMA, most of the mothers were carrying their babies wrapped close to them, with a cloth called a *rebozo*. We seldom heard babies or children crying.

After nine years, many Mexican mothers are pushing their babies in strollers. In my opinion, the bonding between the mother and infant is not going to be as close in the future. Having a stroller may be a status symbol for the more affluent young Mexicans.

I wish I had had my Mexican experiences before my own children were born. I would have carried them close to me, not pushing them in the basic stroller I could afford, trying to get the stroller onto the bus while carrying them, having my daughter stand in the basket at the back of the stroller, while sitting my infant son in the front, groceries in my backpack. All right, all right, it wasn't that bad.

I had many, many unforgettable, marvelous experiences every year we were in SMA. I may not have the dates right, but I will never forget these experiences.

1. One of the Mexican cities we visited had a potter doing a display in the square. The potter asked me to do a pot. No one laughed. Whew. But feeling the clay under my hands, having the opportunity to do this…I remember it.

2. On a trip to Veracruz, our group stopped at a well-known coffee shop. You order your coffee; the waiter arrives and pours your coffee into your cup, from up above you.

Are you there gin? It's me, Mary Ann at 80.

3. On this same trip, I hopped on the back of a motorcycle and the driver (I had no idea who he was) zoomed me around and back to my group.

4. In SMA, Ian and I were standing in line at a little movie theatre. We were not talking as we had just had a very small spat. Two women in front of me were talking. One voice was triggering my memories. I looked at her and said, "Linda?" She looked at me and said, "M.A?" Linda C. is one of my college classmates from Wells. She lives in the Berkshires but was in SMA! Unbelievable. We graduated in 1961 and here we are looking at each other and talking in the 2000s.

5. Following up on #4, Ian was interested in two women's paintings of chapels, as he does these paintings too. After a bit of time, he purchased their book, made contact with them and the three wanted to talk some more. He went to their home. As the afternoon progressed, personal history was shared. This artist went to Wells College too!!! A few years after Linda C. and I graduated.

6. Linda C. invited Ian and me to where she was staying to meet a few people. One of the men takes people on Mexican tours. We connected and went with him, and one of our

neighbors to Xilita. It turns out Linda W. is from Wisconsin, which helped us easily bond and she became a very good friend of ours in SMA.

7. In the central SMA square, Ian and I were watching a LONG parade of all the high schools/elementary schools, along with their marching bands. The students do cartwheels, and all kinds of life-threatening jumps etc. on the cement. I sat down next to a young girl on the curb. In Spanish, which I understood, she told me she was cold. I gave her a coat from my tote. She put it on and leaned into me. I loved it. After a while she saw a boy she wanted to connect with, took off the coat, gave it to me, and ran over to him. Her grandmother was behind us and the grandmother patted me on the shoulder.

8. At Easter time, SMA is abuzz. On the 3rd or 4th Easter we were in SMA, we could hardly walk through the main square on Good Friday as there were so many people there. We were in the midst of a large group of Mexicans, so we thought we would use our Spanish and talk to them. It was a family! By the end of our conversation, they invited us to their home for Easter dinner on Sunday. I was to bring dessert for eight. They would pick us up at 5 p.m.

Are you there gin? It's me, Mary Ann at 80.

On Sunday, Ian called the phone number they gave us. *Si, si, la cena.* At 4:45, our house buzzer rang. My Mexican chocolate mousse for eight is ready, we have a bouquet of flowers for the hostess and a bottle of wine.

I let our children know if they don't hear from us ever again this is why.

We got in the car with a lad who looked like he just got his drivers' license and a younger lass! They drove us somewhere. We had no idea where we were going. We reached a huge house, go in, hugs all over, sit down, and had some wonderful chicken mole, prepared differently than we were used to. Yummy. We had no wine as they couldn't find the corkscrew.

Soon, another couple arrived with a child. The child vanished somewhere. The man spoke fairly fluent English, found the corkscrew, and we all had a dram of wine. Most of the mousse was consumed.

After dinner, we had a house tour. They wanted us to take one of their dogs. We said we couldn't. They invited us to their teenager's 15th birthday in the summer (Patricia invited us to her nieces' 15th, too). We would be included with four hundred others. And they said after the party, we could accompany forty some on the bus for further celebrations at the coast. We mentioned we would not be in SMA at this time.

As 8 p.m. approached, it was evident from their behavior we needed to leave. The man who spoke English invited us to stay in their home for a month when we returned and said we would be speaking Spanish by the end of the month. We thanked him and said we would consider it. The hostess wanted to know if she could keep the mugs the mousse was in and I told her we were renting our home and needed to return the mugs, but she could keep the uneaten mousse. She did.

I let them know we would be back in September when both Ian and I have birthdays and they would be invited to our birthday party. They all burst into laughter. I asked why they were laughing. We were told if this happened, there would be forty people in our house! GREAT!

We were driven back to our home without any problems. We thanked them, got out of the car, and went into our home. I said to Ian, "What is their name?" Ian said, "I don't know." Woe is me. We had their phone number. I asked Laura to call them as we wanted to send them a "thank you" note but didn't know how to spell their name. She didn't call. This not calling may be a cultural "no-no" I didn't understand.

Every time Ian and I were in the mall, we looked for the hostess, as she said this is where she works. We never found her. But this special Easter was a truly treasured experience for Ian and me.

9. There are phenomenal concerts in SMA all year long. *Pro Musica* finds first class musicians from all over the world to perform here. And recently, a children's orchestra began. Our musical teacher, Jesus, is part of helping to get this youth orchestra going.

Are you there gin? It's me, Mary Ann at 80.

Ian and I found the concerts were one of the drawing cards for us to be in SMA. The concerts cost about $14 CAD! They are held in St. Paul's church which has great acoustics, so microphones are not necessary.

One of the most exciting concerts we've seen twice is Elizabeth Pitcairn playing the Stradivarius "red violin." Her grandfather, who is an heir to Felix Mendelssohn, gave the red violin to her when she was sixteen. He was at an auction and paid a good chunk of money for it. She knew she had to measure up to the instrument she was given. She certainly did in my opinion.

10. One year we arrived on Friday and were having company for dinner on Saturday. I went to the Mega Store to get groceries and Ian went to the liquor store to refill our supplies. I got out of the cab, and walked directly to the shopping carts. I did not see the well-marked step in front of me and fell flat on my face. Two Mexican women came running over to me, asked if I wanted an ambulance, could I stand up, etc. I stood up, thanked them, limped to the cart, and figured if I could walk, I could get home by cab. Which I did. There was blood on my elbow, but nothing was broken. Whew.

11. Another pleasant evening, Ian and I were returning to our home from a delightful dinner with neighbors. We were holding hands as we walked. He said, "Oh, look at the moon." I looked up at the moon, missed the curb in front of me and fell down, bringing him down on top of me. An elderly Mexican man came running towards us to help us up. Ian and I were both laughing as I didn't think either of us was hurt. We thanked *el señor* who must have wondered about our sanity.

Ian wears a Mexican leather bracelet that fastens with a metal anchor shaped piece around his wrist. This anchor had jabbed into his arm, causing a good deal of bleeding. I washed the cut and put most of our Band-Aids on his arm. The following day, he stopped in at *La Farmacia* and the kind druggist sprayed his arm with a disinfectant, and put a huge bandage on it.

12. I took a taxi to a local dentist to have my teeth cleaned. Taxi fares are usually forty pesos and we give the driver fifty pesos. The driver asked me if I wanted him to wait. I thought this was very nice of him, as the dentist's office was a bit off the main drag where the taxis are. The teeth cleaning took a little over an hour and the cab driver was there when I exited the dental office. I got in the taxi and gave him my home address. Our street is one way and he was approaching it from the wrong way. Since he had been kind enough to wait for me, I decided to tip him nicely. At the top of our street, I told him to stop and I would walk to our door. I gave him one-hundred pesos and could not get out of the taxi as my door was locked. He said, "No, three-hundred pesos." If looks could kill, there would be one dead Mexican taxi driver. Fortunately, I had two-hundred more pesos. My fuming was unnecessary...three-hundred pesos is close to $21 CAD! And I learned that having a taxi wait for you costs a lot of money.

13. My Vancouver friend, Elsie, was visiting us. Stephen and Lorne invited the three of us to dinner. I wore a snazzy top over some cool jeans. As we were walking halfway to their home, the SMA skies opened up and absolutely soaked us. We arrived looking like three drowned rats. Even Stephen got soaked coming down the short lane to open the door for us to come into their lovely home.

Lorne insisted we wear three of his shirts and he put our clothes in the clothes dryer. It was a fantastic meal in a very relaxed atmosphere! The temperature was warm enough that our bottom halves dried out before we left. I don't remember if it was raining on our way home, but our tops were dry and warm as we left.

During our early years in SMA, we went to see a rug hooking industry formed and supported by an American woman, Charlotte B.

This impoverished Mexican community began to flourish under her guidance, tours, and sales. Charlotte solicits free materials from Americans. She has these materials placed in racing cars coming into Mexico and then she receives the material "free of charge" to give to the women in this community to hook so they can make some financial opportunities for their community.

Each item they hook is different. They make placemats, doormats, wall hangings, etc.

Part of the rug hooking tour includes a lesson in their language from an elder lady.

When we were there the first time, this lady had broken her hip, so was lying down.

She did not have a wheelchair, nor was there one for her in her community. The cost for her to receive appropriate medical attention was too expensive for her or her community.

However, she was a great language teacher and did not complain about her pain.

The community then provided lunch for the tour participants. They taught us to make corn tamales, drink cucumber water and I can't remember what else. While we were eating, we heard a lot of squealing animals. I asked what this was about. Apparently, nearby pigs were being slaughtered.

There was going to be a wedding the following day. We were graciously invited to the wedding.

At the wedding, tequila bottles are set on each table, food is abundant, lots of dancing and toasting. I would have just loved to attend this event, but I was concerned about how Ian and I would get home.

When friends visited us, I often took them on this tour, and I got to know Charlotte. The year we returned to Vancouver for Christmas, I brought twenty hot pad sized hooked parts and sold them, well over the price asked in SMA and returned the money to the community.

Our first time on this tour, our bus driver was Daniel. He gave us his card for future use. Whenever we came or left SMA, we would use Daniel's drivers. His business vastly improved over the time we were in SMA.

He arranged a fantastic trip for us to see the Cañada de la Virgen pyramid with one of the original excavators, followed by a local luncheon afterward. When we got to the top of the pyramid, there was still an ancient corpse lodged in a small enclosure.

Daniel took a group of us to see the monarch butterflies. This trip was a religious experience for me. After you arrive at the huge park, you have a choice of how you want to get to where the monarchs are: you can walk or ride a horse. Ian walked; I rode. The trunks of the trees were almost orange with the thousands of butterflies nestled on them. There were numerous signs in the area for silence. It was hard for me to believe some of these monarchs flew from Canada. The monarch butterfly population is dwindling as the milkweed they feed on in the U.S. is being destroyed.

Daniel couldn't believe I didn't know how to make chili rellenos. So, Daniel took Ian and me to the grocery store he uses to buy the supplies for their rellenos.

He asked me to get the chilies. I obviously did not know which chilies to select. He threw my choices back into the bin and told me the kind of chilies I needed to get.

He drove us to his home.

We met his lovely wife, Nellie, and two young children, Ian and Valentina. We brought two books for their children. I sat reading to them in Spanish. They didn't complain.

Nellie and the men in the kitchen started cooking. We began all of these procedures around noon and wound up eating at 5 p.m. It was great fun and tasted wonderful.

Daniel then called Uber to take us home!

When our children and grandchildren visited at Christmas, Daniel arranged tours for them. Steve and Holly still talk about it. Daniel's sister prepared a typical Mexican Christmas meal for us. I think we received enough food to last to New Year's Eve and beyond.

A few times over the years, Nellie and Daniel were able to join us socially. On one occasion, I served a beverage called *Agua de Jamaica* and a jicama appetizer. The drink is very popular in Mexico, adding sugar and water to the flower petals and boiling them. The drink becomes a lovely maroon color. It is very healthy for you. When I served the appetizer, Daniel told me it is best when served with lime slices. He was totally correct.

In the fall, there is a blessing of animals in many churches.

There is a major horse blessing in San Martín.

Are you there gin? It's me, Mary Ann at 80.

Daniel arranged for a driver to take us there. There were over three-thousand horses. This is a picture of a few of the horses. They are blessed by the priest of the church. Most riders and families camp on the surrounding grounds until it is time to have their horse blessed. They come from miles around.

As we traveled to and from San Martín, we saw many horses and riders coming and going from this area.

The owners are not competitive with one another. St. Paul's, in SMA, has a blessing of the animals. Church members bring their cats, dogs, and rabbits.

Over the nine years we've known Daniel, he never once raised the cost of having us driven between Mexico City and SMA. Even with our last trip and six suitcases. He said he didn't raise our prices as we brought him other business. To me, this is another example of the kind, gentle way the Mexican people we know act.

Several Halloweens ago, my friend Linda W. asked me to come to a preschool to see the children's costumes.

She and other St. Paul's Church members helped start this preschool for poverty-stricken Mexican children. I thoroughly enjoyed this trip. The children were darling, the Day of the Dead display quite impressive and it was fun dancing with the little ones.

The preschool was in operation for just over ten years. All of the children in the preschool are from the poorest Mexican families, mostly with single mothers.

Ian and I chose to support two of the three-year olds for three years. This picture is the first time we saw them. They were performing at St. Paul's for a Christmas pageant.

No one did any research about the graduates of this preschool.

This became my cup of tea.

I developed a simple questionnaire for preschool parents of children about to graduate with the help of Vancouver friends Joyce, Elizabeth, and Lisa.

One mother needed to have the principal read the Spanish questions to her before she could answer them.

The principal, and a woman I was working with, decided to have an open house for preschool graduates. They advertised this invitation on the radio.

I developed another simple questionnaire for high school students whom I hoped would be in attendance.

I wondered how many who attended this preschool would still be in school and attend the open house.

What a surprise for me. There were thirty-four attendees at this open house from several elementary schools! And four girls from high schools!

What an honor for the preschool to have this attendance. The preschool continues to have this open house every year. It is my opinion this continued contact with the students will keep the young people in school.

I gave preschool parents the questionnaire two years in a row. The third year, no one contacted me to do this and visa-versa, so no more data.

This preschool joined with a daycare centre and they may not need any more data. All the parents were and are totally grateful for the financial and emotional support they and their children receive.

Some SMA mothers withdrew their children from daycare as being apart from their infants "didn't work" for them.

In the fall of 2019, I observed a preschool classroom of five and six-year olds, once a week, for three months. The kindness, love, laughter, and support from the teacher to the children and between the children was overwhelming for me. The teacher wanted to know if Ian and I had a Christmas tree and how we celebrated Christmas. Ian and I donated a box of crayons and a pad of drawing paper for each student in the class to use over the Christmas holidays. The teacher had each child do a picture for me. I treasure these pictures. They were making Rudolph headdresses for a Christmas show.

Every February, SMA has a Writers' Conference. One year I decided to participate in it. There were two major authors from Canada, two from the States and two from Mexico. Ian had an art show at a huge B & B during this time and sold several pictures.

The Conference was excellent for me and well attended, as was Ian's art show. I took a weeklong workshop following the Conference from Judyth Hill, the editor of this book! Her energy and enthusiasm encouraged me to continue writing and finishing my autobiography.

Besides all the art courses offered in SMA, there are numerous writing workshops. I participated in several of them over the years. Ian and I enjoyed becoming friends with the Co-Director of the Writers' Festival and her husband, and we are sorry we didn't connect with them earlier in our SMA visits.

I could go on and on about our travels, learning, enjoying people, and events in SMA. This chapter is a mere snapshot of our fantastic nine years in SMA, thanks to the invitation from our friends, Stephen and Lorne to come to SMA.

This is what happens when you retire and "get on with your life."

CHAPTER 18

Is Retirement Fun?

To me "drink responsibly" means don't spill it.
~ Seen on T-shirt

THE ANSWER IS YES: if you plan for it! When I retired, as I stated before, I was on the BC Provincial P.E.O. Board. This meant I stressed about, met, and enjoyed many interesting and challenging goals.

Before Ian retired, he wanted to learn to play the guitar, travel, learn to speak Spanish, and become a painter. He plays the guitar, writes, and speaks Spanish, using a few tenses. He is now an artist with a web site, taking other art courses, has an art bank account, and is having art shows in Vancouver.

We've travelled to numerous countries, before and after we retired. Both of us enjoyed our travels for a variety of reasons.

Ian and I learned a lot about cultures that are very different from what we had known. We ate new foods, we saw historical places we previously learned about in books, we met people who spoke a little English so we were able to communicate with each other, and we gained a broader understanding of the struggles their countries had, their strengths, and an appreciation of their art.

Are you there gin? It's me, Mary Ann at 80.

I so appreciated Ian (well, Ian and our travel agent, P.E.O. Wendy) making all the travel arrangements for us.

We traveled to Russia (tasted great homemade vodka), Finland (purchased award-winning gin), Holland (love our Delft), France, England (family), Scotland, Austria, Germany, Italy, Japan, Malta (great tour guide), Greek Islands (once with girlfriends, once with husband), Mexico, Costa Rica (once with son, once with husband), Belize, Croatia, Denmark, Sweden (once with daughter, once with husband), U.S.A., Poland, St. Lucia, Grenada, Bermuda, Cuba, and Belgium. We don't think we need to travel anymore, other than finding out more about B.C.!

Now, Ian and I will explore British Columbia more deeply. And we want to learn more about our First Nations' populations.

Before I retired, I had the opportunity to go to Hong Kong and Beijing, China with two professional friends. It was a fantastic experience for me. I remember being in Tiananmen Square and seeing a Starbucks Coffee Shop! The three of us bought a cup of coffee and sat on the curb drinking it. I paid a small amount to use the "best" toilet. It had a heated seat and free toilet paper.

The one thing I never experienced is a safari to see wild animals in South Africa (SA). Ian's brother and sister-in-law lived in SA for many years when we were first married. We were unable to find the time due to our professional responsibilities or the dollars to visit them. I'm sorry we didn't do this.

Helping to organize the UBC P.E.O. BQ Chapter on campus, taking violin lessons, playing with the Brock House Orchestra and Chamber Group, being on the Brock House Membership Committee, keeping in touch with children, grandchildren, other relatives, and friends, being part of the 'Dream Group," exercising, and being a good wife keeps me busy. Housekeeping rates very low in my activity level.

Ian and I've made good friends in our condo. Ian and I keep meeting other condo residents, talking to them in the elevator and lobby, enjoying their company and conversation. This keeps our social life active on a weekly basis.

It is so important to keep social contacts whether you are young or old or in midlife. From the research I've read, this is what it's all about. If you want to have a good "old life" keep in touch with friends/family and keep learning.

From my perspective, I don't think there is any formula for this. Just do it.

P.E.O., obviously, is significant for me. When a woman is a P.E.O, as she ages, her chapter supports her and her partner.

Ian and I clicked when we met. We are heading towards our 39th wedding anniversary. We haven't seriously discussed how we will celebrate our 40th or 50th.

I'm not sure how I will cope without him if he dies before me. He hasn't said how he will cope if I die before him. I'm sure you are all anxiously awaiting our comments.

I think these are topics all partners need to discuss and make plans for, to save your children from having to deal with this, when they are grieving your loss.

My parents had everything in order when they died. My sister and I had little to do, other than grieving the loss of our parents and sorting out their few remaining possessions.

Their Wisconsin lawyer, their friend, had their assets in line for my sister and me.

Hopefully our loyal bank person will do the same for our children/grandchildren.

Actually, after my father died, I was in his nursing home room and the phone rang. It was a reporter from the Milwaukee Journal who followed his professional career and read his obit. I wondered how on earth this reporter had his phone number at the nursing home.

I found papers my father wrote about his life for his grand-daughter, Julie. I read this to the reporter. The following day there was a wonderful tribute to him in the Journal and a Des Moines, Iowa newspaper. I would have loved to have found this article to share in this book.

My life has always been interesting. I've been extremely fortunate to have had exceptional opportunities in my work, with my children, in my marriage to Ian, my friendships, and most activities I've participated in. My only regret is mentioned in Chapter 8, but this too was interesting!

As I think about my future, I figure I have twenty years left to enjoy our family, the friends we have, and to get a dog. Ian is not quite on the same page.

The sad part of aging is losing family members and friends. I remember my mother saying there would be no one at her funeral service as all her friends died. The children of her friends were at her memorial service along with her P.E.O. sisters and family. It was a wonderful event, celebrating the lives of both my mother and father.

Marriages, births, and job opportunities are a thing of the past which I enjoy in my memories.

Dealing with the loss of my family and friends is a stage in life I need to adjust to. I am very blessed to know my relatives, P.E.O. Sisters, and Condo friends will be supportive of me.

Epilogue

At my funeral take the bouquet off my coffin,
and throw it into the crowd to see who is next.
~ Seen on T-shirt

AFTER MY PARENTS DIED, I realized there was so much about their lives I never asked them about, and I was never told. I decided to write my autobiography, as I wanted my children and grandchildren to learn more about the events in my life, the various stages of my life, and my belief system.

In writing this book, I took several writing courses over several years. Over time, I received many benefits: I developed friendships; I discovered more facts about our relatives; I became a better writer; I became grateful for the values my parents demonstrated to me as I was growing up; and I almost learned how to use a comma.

The patience and support I received from my editor and publisher kept me writing to completion.

During this book-writing process, I thought a good deal about the strength, love, and encouragement I received from my husband through our thirty-nine years of marriage.

Ian and learned to stop arguing about everything and we are grateful we have each other. I've had a very good life, and I look forward to many more years to come, including maybe writing *My Post-Eighty Years Old Autobiography*!

Mary Ann Carter

About the Author

SOMETIMES I LOOK IN the mirror and I am startled to see my mother looking back at me. My college roommate, Cricket, and life-long friend, Claire, both, independently saw a recent picture of me and both said, "You look just like your mother!"

I wonder if my daughter, Holly, will look like me when she is as old as me. Will my granddaughters, Sophie and Julia, look like me when they are eighty years old?

My life was/is full of strong, rewarding friendships, and not-so-strong or rewarding friendships. I imagine this is the same for the rest of you. I have a few regrets, some of which I haven't written about in this book.

The encouragement friends and family gave me to study for my bachelors, masters and doctoral degree opened up so many wonderful opportunities, interests, and friendships for me. And my studies certainly helped me understand myself and to have better thoughts about myself.

I think enjoying what one owns, personal talents one shares, loving each other, being kind to all, and finding out about new possibilities for yourself is what life is all about, with, of course, a big learning curve along the way!